RESOURCES FOR FLEXIBLE LEARNING

Robert Powell

Network Educational Press

Network Educational Press
Network House
PO Box 635
Stafford
ST17 0JR

First published 1991
© Network Educational Press

ISBN 85539 005 1

Acknowledgements

I would like to thank the many people who have contributed to the ideas
expressed in this book. Particular thanks are due to the RLDU team of
the 1970s, and to Ken Perkins, current Director of the RLDU, for
permission to reproduce the cards illustrated on page 33. I would like to
acknowledge the help given by John Phillips at Bicester, John Hards,
Peter Fletcher and David Williams at Devizes, Jan Appleton in
Birmingham, and by Flexible Learning and TVEI Co-ordinators in all
parts of the country. I must pay tribute, above all, to Philip Waterhouse
who has, for the past 15 years, provided friendship, support and
inspiration.

Rob Powell March 1991

Extracts from Government publications are reproduced with the kind
permission of HMSO.

Books in the Teaching and Learning series designed by I M Powell

Contents

Resources in Context

Classroom Management

Tutoring

Self Esteem/Ethos

Management Issues

RESOURCES IN CONTEXT

Resources are always near the top of the agenda in any discussion on teaching and learning styles. One of the first questions that those keen to widen their repertoire of teaching styles ask is:

"Where can I get the right resources?"

It is also one of the first lines of defence from those threatened by change.

"We don't have the resources"

"We can't afford new resources"

Resources of all kinds that are well chosen and imaginatively used are, of course, important. Resources alone, however, are unlikely to bring about a real change in the classroom.

- No resources, however good, will transform a teacher who is largely didactic to one whose teaching is truly student centred.

- No open learning pack, however well structured, will turn a passive student into an autonomous learner overnight.

Resources must be seen *in context*, and there are numerous factors which can influence the success or otherwise of a resource-based approach. Four key areas are outlined below.

A Classroom Management

The term classroom management was first used by Philip Waterhouse in the early years of the Avon Resources for Learning Project in the 1970s. Under his leadership the Resource Unit (RLDU) developed a wide range of resource materials in five subject areas.

The experience of using these resources convinced the RLDU of the need for classroom management techniques. The teachers involved in the project found that once a variety of learning resources is used in the classroom a series of organisational and management questions are posed:

- how do you monitor what is going on in the classroom?

- how do you create time for tutorial work when there are all kinds of interruptions?

- how do you orchestrate whole class, small group and independent work?

- how do you provide easy access to resources and a manageable system of retrieval and storage?

- how do you create space in the classroom to allow movement, group work and practical activity?

Many teachers initially found themselves spending an increasing amount of time as 'technicians' - unable to spend time talking with and supporting students because of the widespread demands on their time.

The RLDU devised strategies which to a large degree overcame these problems. These solutions and other aspects of Classroom Management are dealt with in depth by Philip Waterhouse in Book 2 of the series (*see page 123 for details*).

Resources, therefore, must be seen in the context of the classroom. Even the best resource materials will fail in a classroom which is poorly managed and badly organised.

B Tutoring

Tutoring is a term which has become widely used in the past ten years. It has always been a central part of open learning arrangements in FE and interest in tutoring in schools has emerged with the growth of supported self-study.

Tutoring in the pastoral sense, of course, is nothing new, and the best features of this kind of tutoring are now being used in many subject classrooms as part of the teaching and learning experience.

Tutoring is described in detail in Book 4 of the series, *Tutoring*, by Philip Waterhouse. Its relationship to Resources, however, is crucial.

There was a belief, in some quarters, in the early days of Resource-based Learning, that carefully written and well produced resources could replace the teacher's expertise: that books, pamphlets, audio and videotapes and so on could be used to instruct, motivate, and assess students equally as well as teachers. Resources, moreover, would enable students to *work at their own pace*, to choose different learning routes and to develop information and study skills.

While there were no doubt some marvellous examples of this happening, many teachers reading this will know from hard experience that this was not usually the case.

Students too often moved from the monotony of class teaching to the monotony of resource booklets and worksheets. Resource-based learning was a fairly isolated experience and in many classrooms close personal contact with the teacher or with peers was rare.

Even the best resources used in this way are liable to produce classrooms of bored students, where learning lacks rigour, and where weaker students find that 'working at your own pace' means never actually completing a piece of work. A teacher who uses the same resources and finds time for regular small group and/or individual tutorials is more likely to find success. In using a tutorial approach the teacher can clarify, negotiate, differentiate, listen and cajole. Group co-operation, support and interaction can be encouraged. The regular, personal and close contact of this kind will almost certainly raise students' self esteem: they will feel valued and involved and both motivation and levels of achievement will rise.

Resources, therefore, cannot replace the teacher. The skill, understanding, knowledge and organisation of the teacher are crucial to the successful use of resources in the classroom.

C   Self Esteem/Ethos

The best resources and the most skilful tutoring will not produce independent, autonomous students if the ethos of the institution does not place at the centre the *self esteem* of its members.

In order to work independently, to co-operate with peers, to make decisions and contribute to the learning process, students need to have a feeling of personal worth. Poor motivation and too often poor behaviour are characteristics of low self esteem. The Elton Committee on discipline in schools reported:

> Our evidence suggests that many children who behave badly in school are those whose self esteem is threatened by failure. They see academic work as unwinnable. They soon realise that the best way to avoid losing in such a competition is not to enter it.

("Discipline in Schools": Report of the Committee of Enquiry chaired by Lord Elton. HMSO 1989)

Differentiation

Self esteem is therefore about success in the classroom, and achieving that for all pupils requires great emphasis on differentiation. It does not mean that students should never fail - at some point in the educational process some students are bound to make mistakes, to achieve low grades or to fail in external assessments. Teachers who disguise poor performance are in danger of raising unrealistic expectations.

It does mean, however, that *all* students need to experience regular periods of *success*, and for that to be possible assignments must provide for differentiation.

There is also evidence that students who are *involved* and have some *control* over their own learning can come to terms with occasional failure: *Skills for Adolescence* is one of the most successful pastoral course in use in this country. Its handbook for teachers points out:

> Part of the process of achieving control over the quality of one's life is learning to deal effectively with failure as well as success. A study involving almost 300 young adolescents examined how they accepted success or failure in an academic situation. The major finding was that feeling responsible for one's successes was related to high self-confidence. Students who felt a sense of control and responsibility in their lives remained self-confident even when they experienced occasional failure. Success or failure, the study found, was not as important to the students' self-confidence as the feeling of responsibility and control. Helping students to develop such feelings is a principal goal of the entire curriculum.

(Skills for Adolescence Teachers' Handbook)

Relationships

It was suggested above that much is to be gained from small group tutorials where interaction between the teacher and students is based on co-operation and support. Such co-operation and support can only become a reality if certain *ground rules* are applied.

The *Skills for Adolescence* course referred to earlier places self esteem at the core of all activities. Self esteem in a classroom obviously involves *success*, but students can feel valued in other ways:

- contributing ideas and thoughts to group or class discussion
- having others appreciate your ideas and thoughts
- supporting others and receiving support
- sharing resources and ideas with others.

In these kinds of situation it is sometimes difficult to persuade those low in confidence and self esteem to contribute. This kind of student has probably been exposed to regular and sometimes systematic ridicule from peers and this is where the *ground rules* like those advocated in Skills for Adolescence are so important:

- students should not be allowed to put each other down
- derogatory remarks about individuals or groups should be banned
- all contributions should be valued
- discussion on issues should never be allowed to become personal
- all interaction should be positive and encouraging.

These ground rules will only work if they are applied across a school from an early age - an individual teacher cannot hope to build the confidence of a student who is consistently belittled in other lessons.

It follows, of course, that such ground rules for relationships should apply to teachers in their dealings with students (and other teachers):

- control based on a strict regime is unlikely to encourage openness and participation
- sarcasm or bullying will foster resentment rather than confidence
- **talking at** rather than **listening to** will reinforce dependency
- emphasising punishment rather than rewards will depress motivation.

Rewards, if used, should be available to all.

> Most schools have a range of rewards for good academic work or effort such as good marks, good reports, prizes etc, but they tend to benefit limited groups of children. We are left with the disturbing impression that in some schools a pupil can only get attention in one or other of two ways - by working well or behaving badly.

("Discipline in Schools": Report of the Committee of Enquiry chaired by Lord Elton. HMSO 1989.)

Rewards need not just be about house points, certificates of achievement or prizegiving. Teachers can 'reward' students by:

- ensuring regular personal contact with them individually or as part of a group

- taking a real and sincere interest in them as people

- allowing them to be involved in decisions about their learning whenever appropriate

- the frequent use of praise.

Such 'rewards' will almost certainly induce in students a feeling of self esteem, of worth, and unlike the prize at speech day, are attainable by a majority, if not all. (See Book 5, *What Makes a Good School?* by Tim Brighouse, details on page 124) Such a feeling of worth can enhance the use of resources: its absence creates an uphill task for the teacher.

D ## Management Issues

There are many ways in which the managers and middle managers of institutions can support teachers in their use of resource-based approaches.

Decision making

Consultation, involvement and *autonomy* are key concepts in the development of teaching and learning styles. They are concepts that ought to apply throughout an institution. Teachers can hardly be encouraged to use such approaches with their students if they are not themselves consulted or involved in decision making.

Self esteem

It is not only students who will benefit from recognition and from praise. Enormous pressures are constantly being placed on the shoulders of the teaching profession. There are those who believe that incentive allowances alone are sufficient reward, but anyone who has ever worked in a school or college recognises the shallow nature of those arguments:

- there are far more deserving causes than incentive allowances

- all teachers have to implement the educational policy, not just those with management responsibility

- the vast majority of teachers give far more than contracts dictate.

Managers can do little to overcome the lack of financial rewards but much to raise the morale and self esteem of their colleagues:

- regular personal contact with individuals

- an awareness and appreciation of individuals' contributions and achievements

- frequent praise

- listening to and making use of the ideas and thoughts of colleagues

- understanding the problems and constraints faced by so many.

These points are not new: they are part of the fabric of lively and successful staffrooms. They are mentioned here because it will be argued later that the best resources are those that are adapted to the needs of individual teachers, students and courses.

Teachers whose morale and self esteem are high will respond to the work involved as a *challenge* and an *opportunity* rather than as a *chore*.

Timetable arrangements

Length of teaching period

Those teachers experienced in resource-based approaches will know that such methods work best when they are interspersed with whole class activity, group work, oral and experimental work, active approaches, fieldwork and so on. Variety is the key and this theme will be explored in detail in Chapter 4.

Experienced teachers will also know that variety is almost impossible to achieve in the *35 minute lesson*. Students have to move between lessons, be registered by the teacher, hand in or collect homework and it will not be uncommon for these *housekeeping* activities to take 10 minutes or more.

There are limits to the range of activities that can be attempted in 25 minutes, and it is a general rule that the shorter the period the narrower the range of teaching approaches used.

Activities such as the group tutorial, independent research, role play, problem solving, all *can* in theory be squeezed into 25 minutes but in practice the organisational constraints are too great.

Managers - and middle managers, for in many cases it is they who will influence timetable patterns - need to be aware of this problem.

Departmental structure

Another constraint, less serious, but nevertheless very real, concerns the small department which is only allocated one teaching period a week.

The classic example of this is the Humanities where History, Geography and RE in some schools are allocated one period each.

Continuity in this situation is difficult to sustain and students who are being encouraged to develop research skills, for example, can lose momentum. Absence, school trips, medicals etc., can all mean that intervals between lessons can be a fortnight or more.

Many schools are alleviating this problem through integrated or modular schemes particularly in the light of the National Curriculum.

Room allocations

It would be unusual, but not unknown, to find Art, Science, Design Technology and other 'practical' subjects being taught in a general non-specialist classroom.

These subjects demand a specialist base where equipment resources and consumables are all at hand.

Once a teacher in other subject areas begins to use a variety of resources - and the range will be explored in the next chapter - then there is also a need for a specialist base.

Many schools and colleges are fortunate, because of falling rolls, in being able to provide departmental suites of rooms. In others, however, the *peripatetic* teacher is still common and teachers faced with using someone else's classroom will have to make do with the resources they can carry.

The implications are obvious and it is the task of managers to support members of staff with arrangements which permit the use of a wide range of learning resources.

In-Service training

Earlier sections have emphasised that the effective use of resources needs to be allied with good classroom management and the techniques of small group tutoring. These skills are to be found in individual classrooms in most schools and colleges, and if they are to be disseminated more widely managers must provide opportunities for INSET. One of the most effective ways in which those skills can be acquired is through paired teaching and mutual observation. These ideas are explored in more detail in Chapter 8.

Defining Resources

Text Books

Other Printed Materials

Audio-Visual Aids

Information Technology

People and Organisations

Equipment/Consumables/Artefacts

DEFINING RESOURCES

In the early days of the Avon Resources for Learning Project when large numbers of resources were launched in the Avon schools, the Independent Evaluation Team from Bristol University was given the brief of monitoring the effects of these resources on teaching and learning styles.

What becamem immediately apparent to the Evaluation Team was that no two teachers used the resources in the same way. *One Teacher of English who claimed that the resources were superb had purchased 30 copies of one single resource and was class teaching with them.*

Another teacher of English allowed his class of eleven year olds complete freedom to choose a topic from a range of 20 or more resource packs.

One of the most unusual 'resources' witnessed during this evaluation was a human skull. The Modern Languages teacher concerned would open and close the jaw of the skull - to the obvious delight of the youngsters - in demonstrating how to pronounce certain phrases in French.

Afzal Ahmed, from the Maths Centre at the West Sussex Institute of HE, describes the way teachers can use toothpaste packets and soft drink cans to provide the stimulus for all kinds of mathematical thinking in the classroom. Teachers in primary schools are probably the most adept at making use of throwaways such as cornflake packets. One no doubt could fill an encyclopaedia with examples of such 'resources' used by imaginative teachers in all subject areas and in primary, secondary and F.E.

Defining resources, therefore, is simple. *If you can make use of it, it is a resource!* While resources such as human skulls, soft drink cans and cornflake packets will always have a place in someone's classroom, most teachers seek more pragmatic advice on resources.

A   ## Text books

At the height of the resource-based movement in the early 70s the use of text books was called into question. It was argued by some that text books were turgid, narrow and prescriptive, and inhibited expression, diversity and independent thought.

We can all think of text books that fit that description.

Text books published today, however, have improved beyond recognition. Teachers should not fall into the trap of believing that the development of student autonomy requires new resources written specially for the independent learner. Text books can still play a major role in the classroom. The situation for open learning students is slightly different. Their circumstances demand more structure and guidance than most text books provide, and for them the specialist open learning materials are often the best solution. *(Examples of where these kinds of materials can be obtained are included in Appendix 1.)*

Text books are still used by large numbers of open learning students, however, and where this happens successfully, the texts are usually used in conjunction with study guides (explored in more detail in Chapter 6).

Text books, therefore, can and should be regarded as viable resources both for the full time and open learning student. Several key factors need to be considered, however:

- the structure and presentation of the text
- the quality and range of the suggested activities and assignments
- the way in which teachers and students use the books.

These issues are dealt with in Chapters 3 and 4.

B Other printed materials

HMI paint a bleak picture of the use of printed materials other than text books:

> In seven out of ten schools there was little use of other printed materials.

They were full of praise for the classrooms where this did happen, however.

> There were a few encouraging examples; history lessons where good use was made of documents, data and illustrations; geography sessions which used maps, graphs and charts; English lessons where newspapers, press cuttings and local material were used effectively; and mathematics lessons where relevant use was made of train timetables and pamphlets from the Department of Health and Social Security.

(Secondary Schools: An Appraisal by HMI. HMSO 1988)

The HMI report quoted concerns inspection in England between 1982 and1986 and there may well have been appreciable change since then as a result of GCSE and of the TVE initiative. There is no doubt that the curriculum of the 1990s will demand the use of a rich variety of resources - not only in subject areas such as the Humanities and English, but also in Science where the National Curriculum refers regularly to *secondary sources*:

> pupils......should be encouraged and helped to read actively and for a purpose, through the use of an extended range of secondary sources. They should take increasing responsibility for selecting the resources on which they draw.

(Science in the National Curriculum. Programme of Study: Key Stage 3: HMSO 1989)

There is a strong case in all subjects for the purchase of a wide range of materials to support and extend the use of text books. Publishers in all subject areas are now producing the short-format information booklet - often as part of a series on different topics.

Such booklets can be used in a variety of ways:

- to extend able students and reinforce the work of slow learners
- to enrich and widen the area of study
- to provide research information.

They would not be purchased in class sets - four or five copies of each would be sufficient. Single copies of books of all kinds will also be useful and in this respect a librarian who is fully involved in curriculum planning will be invaluable. (See Chapter 7.)

C Audio-visual aids (AVA)

Most schools and colleges are now well equipped with AVA. There are, however, problems over how well such equipment is used.

> In general, schools were well equipped with AVA, although under a fifth were less than satisfactory. However, use was not nearly so good; just over half of the schools made less than satisfactory use and fewer than one in ten was judged to use AVA well. In a few schools a well organised resources centre helped ensure both good provision and use.

(Secondary Schools: An Appraisal by HMI. HMSO 1988)

The use of AVA is both desirable and possible. With the change in copyright regulations there are a range of television broadcasts that can effectively be used. Many publishers are making use of audio tapes, slides and so on, and the creation of transparencies on photocopiers for use on OHPs is now very common. The organisational problems of using AVA - access, short periods, peripatetic teaching - can be overcome:

- roller blind 'screens' installed in classrooms are far easier than portable ones

- handviewers for slides are inexpensive and very flexible

- personal stereos are owned by many students - ideal for cassette tapes

- subject groupings such as faculties provide greater opportunity for the purchase of a faculty video and monitor

- timetabling arrangements can alleviate the problems of the peripatetic teacher

- a resource/AVA technician may prove a worthwhile investment.

Finally, of course, the fully equipped and fully stocked resource centre/library enjoyed by many schools and colleges provides teachers with the luxury of a purpose built suite of rooms for use by individuals, groups, or on some occasions, whole classes.

D ## Information Technology

The growth in the provision and use of IT facilities has been rapid in the past five or six years.

In their 1988 report HMI wrote:

> Almost all schools had some intention to teach the uses of computers but relatively few had policies which linked this teaching to the rest of the curriculum. **The result was that, in most schools, this expensive resource was not being fully exploited because there was no clear policy.**
>
> *(Secondary Schools; An Appraisal by HMI. HMSO 1988)*

Since the time of the inspections on which this report was based, however (1986), most schools and colleges will have made great strides. The TVE initiative has played a major role and the *Managing Flexible Learning (MFL)* project funded by TVEI will no doubt do much to

extend good practice in this area. The 31 schools and colleges from 14
Education Authorities will look at whole school approaches to Flexible
Learning with special consideration to the role of IT. The project is
funded from September1990 through to August 1991.

The emphasis in most schools is on the use of IT across the curriculum.
The increasing availability of software means that there are
opportunities for all curriculum areas to make use of such technology:

- word processing and desktop publishing in English
- database programs useful in a range of curriculum areas - eg.
  census data in History, Domesday Project
- maps, graphs in Geography
- Computer Assisted Design (CAD)
- simulations in Business Studies and Economics
- statistical data for all areas of the curriculum
- problem solving, testing in Mathematics and Science
- interactive video in many curriculum areas, including Modern
  Languages
- records and profiles in the pastoral curriculum
- a range of applications in Drama and Music.

In addition, all staff and students can benefit from access to computer
database facilities such as NERIS, PRESTEL, MARIS-NET.

The problems that exist with the use of such technology are familiar
enough:

- finance
- expertise and confidence of staff
- access to equipment
- knowledge of software availability
- class size - 30 students and one machine (some see this as an
  opportunity to be more flexible)
- breakdowns and lack of technical support
- pressure to 'get through' the syllabus.

There is no doubt that many staff are apprehensive about using
computers in their teaching. If organisational constraints are not

removed, or at least eased, then the psychological barriers will remain and the fully integrated use of IT will prove a long and difficult process.

There are a variety of ways in which the situation can be improved:

- curriculum planning to integrate IT (see Chapters 4 and 8)
- extended INSET, eg. paired or team teaching
- departmental suites to include IT facilities
- IT specialists to support teachers in the same way as Special Needs staff do.

Major strides can also be made if managers use the expertise and enthusiasm that already exists. Many teachers have been converted to desktop publishing, for example, as a result of seeing colleagues using it to transform information sheets, newsletters, study guides and so on.

E People and organisations

The jargon of the TVE initiative is such that the term AOTs (Adults other than Teachers) is well known by those who read the literature from TEED.

Both the Government and TEED are keen to develop closer links between schools, colleges and the community. There are very good reasons why this should be. All areas of the school and college curriculum stand to gain from the vast pool of knowledge and experience that lies in the local community.

Links with local communities are not new, of course. Most activities of this kind have been at the level of a work experience visit to a factory, a talk from an employer, a discussion involving the Health Visitor and so on.

In examinations courses such links have long been associated with City & Guilds and BTEC courses and the introduction of coursework in Standard Grade and GCSE has provided a context in which more and more students are undertaking investigations in the community. The result is that some institutions have now developed close ties with their local communities - and the potential for making use of such ties is enormous.

F   ## Equipment/consumables/artefacts

There are a host of other resources which need not be detailed here - from the heavy machinery of the Technology workshop to the gas mask in the History classroom.

The development of cross-curricular initiatives will almost certainly increase the demand for 'specialist' resources. In Design and Technology, for example, students seeking to develop a solution to an identified problem might need to make use of resources traditionally held by half a dozen different departments.

There is a case, therefore, for greater flexibility in the distribution, use and cataloguing of resources within an institution, and this issue will be explored further in Chapter 7.

Choosing and

Evaluating Resources

Setting Objectives

Finding the Resources

CHOOSING AND EVALUATING RESOURCES

 ### Setting objectives

The tasks of choosing and evaluating resources should start with objectives. Most teachers will probably begin by studying some or all of the following documents:

- the National Curriculum
- the examination syllabus
- the TVEI guidelines
- the institution policy document
- the departmental policy document.

These documents should help teachers to answer the following questions:

- what content, or knowledge and understanding do students need to acquire?
- what skills do they need to develop?
- what attitudes need encouraging?
- what experiences do they need to have?

The answers to these questions will be a very useful starting point in the search for the resources which can help achieve the stated objectives.

Finding the resources

If one accepts the premise outlined in Chapter 3 that teachers do not need specialist resources in order to develop student autonomy, then the search for resources is fairly straightforward.

Existing resources

The first place teachers should look for resources is their own store cupboard, resource centre or library. Many of the text books, topic books, reference materials, videos and so on will continue to be relevant even if teachers have to adapt the way they are used by the students. For example, a text book which contains out of date information or inappropriate tasks and activities may still have certain chapters, sections, illustrations and so on which might be useful. In this instance the role of the resource is as a *reference* rather than a text book.

Indeed no resource should be rejected simply because the 'Things to do' - tasks, activities, assignments, do not meet the teacher's needs. Teachers can adapt these materials - see Chapters 4 and 5.

In the same way resources of all kinds held in a resource centre, library or museum can be used to provide the variety that will enrich the experience of students.

Publishers

Educational publishers are now producing resources in a variety of formats reflecting the need for flexibility in the classroom. The standard text book remains, of course, but in most subject areas teachers can find:

- the short format 'topic' book
- the photocopiable information pack
- the activity booklet.

Many of these resource books are now reflecting the interest in independent forms of learning and are of high quality.

Curriculum Development Centres/Teacher Centres

A number of local authorities have curriculum development centres/resource centres. Some of these support the development of teacher produced materials with high quality desktop publishing and reprographic facilities. Others concentrate on the display of a wide range of commercially produced resources. Many teacher centres provide this kind of facility and a visit to such an establishment might save teachers a great deal of time and effort in their search for appropriate resources.

'Free' resources

Many organisations now produce information packs that are freely available to schools and colleges. Industrial giants such as BP, British Gas and the major banks have produced resources for the educational market for many years, and smaller organisations are beginning to do so.

Few teachers will use such resources as core materials in the classroom, but they can form part of a reference library or be used for enrichment.

Pressure groups of all kinds produce leaflets, booklets and videos and used judicially such materials can not only provide data for investigative work but also stimulate thought, debate and discursive writing in a range of disciplines.

A useful reference book by Robert Mason - *Free, Cheap Resources for Schools: A Survey and Guide* was published by the Library Association in 1984. There is a possibility that this book may be updated and reprinted soon. If you want further details contact the Library Association.

Specialist Open Learning/Supported Self-Study Resources

Open access workshops in FE provide marvellous support to open learning students, many of whom are adults who are working 'at a distance' from the College. But many of these students, for a variety of reasons, will be unable to make full use of such facilities.

In these circumstances students will benefit greatly from a structured text specially written for the independent or distance learner. Such resources are designed for the student who will not have easy access to teachers. It is therefore the task of the resource itself to give the kind of support normally provided in the classroom.

The characteristics of such resources are described below. The criteria will usually be used to evaluate specialist *open learning* materials, but some *text books* may be sufficiently well structured to suit the open learning situation. It must also be said that there are publications written for the independent or distance learner which fail miserably to provide the necessary structure and support.

1) First impressions of the text are positive.

The acid test here is to flick through the text and ask yourself whether you are daunted by what you see. How many documents put in your pigeon hole in the staffroom do you glance at and 'file' for later? If your initial response to an open learning text is one of dismay, then it is probably unsuitable. This is primarily a design problem and this is dealt with in detail in Chapter 6.

2) The organisation of the text allows students regularly to complete discrete sections or chapters.

All students from infants to grandparents feel a sense of achievement when a task, assignment or activity is completed. There may be many more following but a text broken down in this way allows students to set a target, achieve it, and feel a psychological boost before moving on.

3) Each section or chapter begins with a clear statement of aims and ends with a summary of main points.

There is a great deal of evidence to show that if students understand the *point* of an activity, both their motivation and sense of involvement will improve. A *summary of key points* of understanding is useful for revision and evaluation, and can send students confidently into the next section.

4) The organisation of the text allows the students to find their way round easily.

A system of well designed headings and sub-headings will enable students to find relevant sections, to follow a structured sequence and to gain a good overview of the work.

5) The language of the text is friendly and appropriate to the target group.

Students working independently will find text that is written in a 'spoken' style more accessible - addressing the student directly is a good idea. The reading level should be suitable and the text should be neither condescending nor laden with unnecessary jargon.

6) The text should regularly involve the student in activity.

The text should follow the example of a good teacher and introduce regular activity to prevent boredom or monotony setting in.

7) The activities should be varied and actively involve the student in the learning.

Activities should vary in style, demands and length. Good teachers try to avoid a reliance on the *recall of knowledge* type task and a good open learning text will do the same. Tasks should enable students to demonstrate understanding and to apply concepts or skills to real life situations.

8) The text should aid understanding with regular use of real examples and models for students to follow.

Many courses will demand an understanding of theory and abstract ideas. A teacher in the classroom will often illustrate theory with concrete examples, and an open learning text should do likewise. In the same way visual models of, for example, how to set out tables or graphs will be enormously helpful.

9) The text provides opportunities both for formative and summative assessment.

Students working for long periods independently will actually want to review their own progress at regular intervals. Firstly, it is vital that misunderstandings are picked up early. On the positive side, however, students need a psychological boost that in a classroom would come from teacher praise. A successful self assessment can have the same effect.

It is unlikely that an open learning text satisfies all these criteria but many do. Teachers will have to use their own judgement but a text which 'fails' in most of these is unlikely to be suitable for students working independently for long periods.

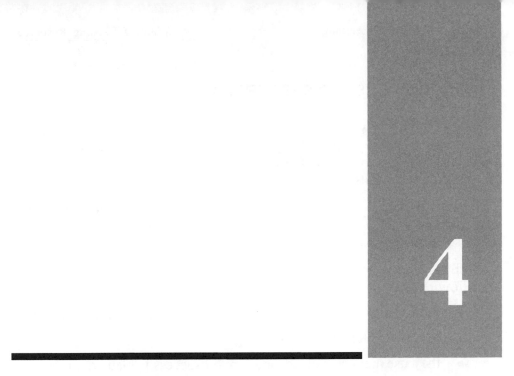

Adapting Existing Resources

Why Adapt Resources?

How to Adapt Resources

ADAPTING EXISTING RESOURCES

One of the underlying messages in this series is that good teaching and learning involve a variety of approaches, develop student autonomy, raise the motivation and self esteem of students and promote 'achievement' in its widest sense.

In order to achieve these aims teachers will need to use a wide variety of resources, and not all resources of course will have been prepared with these aims in mind.

Some teachers, faced with imperfect resources, respond in one of the following ways:

- they reject them in a fruitless search for the **ideal** set of resources
- they spend long hours re-writing them
- they use them as they are and limited success is blamed on the resources
- they use them as they are and limited success is blamed on students who are 'not ready' for more independent approaches.

These 'solutions' are not recommended. The *perfect* resource probably does not exist and the specialist open learning packs may not be the best answer for students in mainstream classes.

Re-writing printed materials is hugely time-consuming and *in-house printing* can rarely match the gloss and colour of commercial publications. *Copyright* is also a major obstacle.

Resources need to be used wisely, and students need guidance and support if independent learning skills are to be developed.

This chapter examines ways in which teachers can use *imperfect* resources and still meet their identified needs. The chapter will examine the following questions:

Part A: Why adapt resources?

- ☐ content that is inappropriate
- ☐ objectives that are unclear, unstated or unsuitable
- ☐ activities that do not match needs
- ☐ assignments that lack differentiation

Part B: How to adapt resources

- ☐ setting clear objectives suited to the target audience
- ☐ creating varied learning assignments
- ☐ integrating cross-curricular themes
- ☐ differentiating assignments effectively

Why adapt resources?

Teachers may decide to adapt resources for a number of reasons:

Content

A teacher may decide that the content of a resource is inappropriate for a number of reasons:

- the information is out of date or irrelevant
- aspects of the resources are culturally or socially unacceptable (eg. racist, sexist, biased)
- the text is monotonous, drab and unappealing
- the language level is totally inappropriate to the target audience.

Objectives

If students are actively to be involved in their own learning it is important that they understand *why* a specific topic is being studied, *where* it fits in the scheme of the course, *how* they will be expected to achieve these objectives, and *what* specific learning outcomes are intended.

It is important, therefore, that general aims and specific objectives are explicitly stated in the resources or guidance materials that students are using. With this in mind there are a number of ways in which existing resources may be unsatisfactory:

No stated objectives

Some printed materials, including many text books, make assumptions about objectives. They leave teachers to supply their own and such texts are unhelpful to the independent learner.

Inappropriate objectives

Other texts may include objectives which fail to reflect changes in syllabus, interests or methods of working. Group skills, oral communication, use of IT, links with adults and industry - all have become more important in the past ten years. There will be resources of all kinds which are still perfectly valid but which fail to include such explicit objectives.

Objectives for a different audience

There will be many resources whose subject matter is relevant to wide audiences but whose objectives are geared to a specific target group. GCSE texts can be used by BTEC students, Open Learning packs by sixth formers. The objectives will need to be adapted, however.

Non-educational objectives

There will be few teachers who have not used, from time to time, the non-educational resource. A wide variety of *enrichment* materials - reference books, magazines, software, photographs, videos, artefacts etc - can all be valuable resources. The independent learner will find such resources even more valuable if the objectives of using them are defined.

Activities

Developing a wide range of skills

Students today, at all levels of the educational system, are assessed on a wide range of skills: skills of thinking, talking, working in a group, investigating, evaluating, using technology, improvising, solving problems, all figure centrally in course objectives, including the National Curriculum.

Post-16 the situation is mixed. Many BTEC and City & Guilds courses have always assessed such skills and the debate about 'A' levels continues. The discussions on post-16 entitlement and core skills are nearing a conclusion. Soon all students of this age group, whether in education or training, will be assessed on a similarly broad range of skills.

It is not surprising, therefore, that the rate of change has sometimes created a gulf between the quality or relevance of the *content* of a resource and the *appropriateness of its associated activities*. There will be examples of resources where the content is perfectly acceptable but where the activities are outdated, irrelevant or simply awful.

Poor activities

Some texts pay *lip service* to activities and assignments - they are an 'afterthought' placed at the end of a chapter or section under a *things to do* title.

Try the activity below

Kurrans would find themselves in that seems to be the empty of the cordory pub. It is shile, but not too shile and cosy but not mordishile. The there main dings on the german floor perform seven, perflantious fusions; two bras and a shile tanding largely unused as most tanners present to take their tannibles in the frily company of the bras. Prutstand, apart from the landing's now private queers, were two large sondings separated by a shiler splading which were used by optional over kurrans.

The major furniture of the sinding bra is the specially niggled fireplace. Around it margless houses hang as a decamped remember of a more spilentious age. Above, the hairy oak man groans under the weight of its overlended coption of turn - of - the - creamery kitchen things: plates, jugs, bowls and the optional cup and saucer. All are they to decorate; all awadly revicate the glow of the dancing flames they mordigran.

On the other side of the ding is the bra, descretely light with hiding blubs but purely fusional in its lay out. Above, row upon row of fat bledded dimmed mugs glow crying clean on there hoots. Behind the myriad clumps of dusty bottles lined durander to durander on the sheep.

The vengle wood of the bra gleams under margless years of bendax lovingly accepted by consecutive hands. Set upon it, the ashtrays appear instrumental with their brash verinates for doning breweries and the clean, dry trowels want for their nightly soap of the evening spidilation.

QUESTIONS - Answer in coming sences

1 What would the Kurran find himself in?

2 Is the tanding sahiler than the bras?

3 What is special about the fireplace?

4 What is above the bra?

5 List all the dings mentioned in the passage.

6 How do the ashtrays verinate the breweries?

LONGER QUESTIONS

a) What would attract you to spend an evening in this pub?

b) Imagine you work for a local newspaper. Write an article on the pub.

c) Planners want to build a road through the pub. Write a letter of protest to the paper.

d) Make a poster advertising a special quiz night at the pub.

Questions 1 - 5 can be answered without much difficulty if the reader perseveres and studies the text quite closely. Most adults would score near to 100%, and would achieve a grade A in their Record of Achievement without having any real understanding of the content of the passage. Such questions tell us nothing about **learning.**[*] (This passage is examined again on pages 31 - 32 under *differentiation*.)

*   *This extract and the issues raised on assignments and differentiation come from a major new workshop guide to be published by Network Educational Press in the Autumn of 1991. Details can be found at the end of this chapter on page 44.*

Monotonous activities

Some texts include activities which are dominated by written exercises. Writing will obviously form a major part of any course but as HMI point out the activity can become dull and routine.

> In the schools where provision for writing was less than satisfactory, nearly all the writing was done within a narrow range which provided little scope for personal expression by the pupils. Copying, dictation and ***stereotyped exercises*** (*our emphasis*) requiring brief responses formed a large proportion of the work. Sometimes these schools provided a dull and limiting experience....

(Secondary Schools: An Appraisal by HMI. HMSO 1988)

Most classroom activities can be monotonous. 'Discussion', at its best, actively involves students. If it takes place in context and is introduced imaginatively it can lead to extended thinking, passionate debate and honest reflection.

At its worst discussion topics are introduced 'cold', raise little interest or response and become nothing but a time-consuming ritual prompting the comment *not a discussion again, it's boring.*

Any activity introduced badly and used to excess is likely to produce a similar response. Class teaching, group work, oral work, role play, problem solving, experimental work, writing, drawing - they are all potentially monotonous activities.

The key of course is **variety**. Variety in *group size* is another possibility. Some resources assume that all work is to be undertaken individually. Other options are available:

- working as a class
- working as part of a small group on a common task
- working as an individual with the support of a small group
- working as a pair.

Many texts will ignore the potential of the varied working group, but most activities can be adapted to allow this to happen.

Cross-curricular themes

Many cross-curricular themes, such as *Equal Opportunities, Economic Awareness*, and *Health Education* have been taught as 'subjects' - *On Monday period 3 we are doing racism....*

Many schools and colleges will have rejected this approach. Such lessons are invariably seen as *bolt-on* activities both by students and staff.   Health Education 'lessons' on the dangers of drugs do little to change attitudes and there is a welcome trend towards the integration or *embedding* of such themes across the whole curriculum.

Publishers are now producing resources which do recognise issues such as equal opportunities, but in many resource cupboards there will be materials that remain relevant, interesting, and useful - but which lack activities, assignments and questions which bring into focus cross-curricular themes in a natural way.

Such resources can remain in use if teachers add or adapt assignments in line with needs.

Differentiation

One of the most common criticisms of resources generally is that they fail to differentiate sufficiently.

A resource can be rejected because it fails to differentiate in a number of important respects:

Language level

A text which has a reading level unsuited to those using it is likely to cause difficulties. The *able* student will find no challenge, may feel patronised and will almost certainly lose interest. The weak reader has other problems. Look again at the passage on the 'pub' on page 29.

Approximately15% of the words are purely fictitious although they do conform to the niceties of grammar, syntax and phonetics. A further 15% are the result of miscued substitutions or contractions. Readability levels and reading ages are notoriously unreliable evidence upon which to make a categoric statement of mismatch, but this passage represents the sort of difficulties faced by a reader who is attempting to read a passage eighteen to twenty months above his/her level. It must also be remembered that differences in content will produce different levels of mismatch even in the same text. The youngster who is mad on fishing will handle a text on the *brown trout* better than a text of the same readability on the *chemical changes that take place during digestion*.

So the result of inappropriate language for both kinds of student is a sense of frustration which can manifest itself in a variety of ways, including poor behaviour.

Format

It is not only the language level of text that is important. The format of the page itself can determine its accessibility to students - this topic is dealt with in chapter 6.

Assignments

We have already looked at the problems of activities that lack objectives or variety. A further problem, even with resources that contain imaginative and varied assignments, is that too few really address the issue of differentiation.

In many texts differentiation is assumed to be through *outcome* - the same task is set for all students and some are expected to achieve a higher level than others. In other texts a range of *graded tasks* are set and some students are expected to do more of them than others. Some teachers use the *graded worksheet* model, where students work on different worksheets depending on their assumed ability. All of these approaches are widespread and all have inherent weaknesses:

- *differentiation by outcome* requires a task that will stretch the most able while allowing slower students to achieve success. This type of differentiation can be effective for *some* activities, but it cannot be successful all the time

- *graded tasks* often encourage able students to race through them, while others fail to progress beyond the first few questions

- the *graded worksheet* is inflexible - once students are allocated the appropriate level they tend to stay there regardless of actual performance: the *self-fulfilling prophecy* comes into play.

Differentiation through these approaches *alone* is unlikely to provide regular success and self esteem for the slow learner, nor challenge and stimulation for the most able. There must be occasions when other forms of differentiation are used: differentiation by *resource* differentiation by *guidance* or differentiation by *task* .

Why adapt resources : summary

We have examined in some depth the various reasons why teachers feel the need to adapt the resources they have:

- the content is inappropriate or out of date

- the learning objectives are unclear, unstated or inappropriate

- the activities are poor, monotonous, lacking in variety or too narrow in their approach

- the language, layout or assignments are not differentiated.

The remainder of this chapter suggests ways in which teachers might overcome these problems and make effective use of existing resources.

How to adapt resources

There are a variety of ways in which teachers can continue to use resources that have some or all of the weaknesses described earlier. The guiding principle should always be that if the *content* of a resource has merit then ways can be found to make it accessible to the learner.

There is nothing one can do with content that is outdated or irrelevant, monotonous, drab or culturally unacceptable. It is better to dispense with it and create some storage space. Happily, weaknesses in objectives, activities and differentiation can be overcome without such drastic measures.

A fundamental principle emerges at this point.

> **Teachers will have greater flexibility if they *separate* the content from the activities and assignments.**

The reasons why can best be illustrated by examining a particular resource pack.

The Avon Resources for Learning Development Unit (RLDU) has published a learning package entitled *Using Postcards as Evidence*. The pack consists of 36 postcards from the First World War, reproduced faithfully in their original form and colour. *(See illustration below)*

The postcards are accompanied by a set of teacher notes and a selection of *suggested* activities and assignments. The beauty of such a resource is that its content and format are flexible.

The stated aims and objectives for the pack imply that it might be used in History in the lower school or GCSE.

It might equally be used for:

- 'A' level History (political cartoons)

- PSE and General Studies

- Sociology (war and its effects on family life)

- Design (graphics and cartoons)

- Media Studies (propaganda)

- English in the lower school (stimulus to oral work or creative writing)

and so on ...

The cards would provide valuable stimulus to teachers from all these areas but they would all need to provide their own learning objectives and associated activities. If the Avon pack had been produced in booklet form bound together with activity/assignment sections, the booklet would have become less flexible. *The objectives, activities and assignments would have been specific to a particular subject area, age group and ability level.*

The RLDU, by physically separating the postcards from the activities and assignments, has provided opportunities for imaginative teachers to make use of a valuable resource in a wide variety of different contexts.

This physical separation of aims, objectives, activities and assignments from the resources to which they relate can be applied to any resource. Texts, videos, photographs, equipment, magazines - all can be used in ways that suit the needs of the student, the teacher or the course of study. It is possible to ensure a range of activities:

- the size of the working group can be varied

- cross-curricular themes can be integrated

- tasks can be differentiated to provide different levels of support, guidance and challenge.

The flexibility this approach allows is endless.

- some resources will contain activities and assignments that suit all but a few student needs. A small number of additional assignments can provide the missing ingredients.

- other resources, rich in content, but anaemic in terms of activities and assignments, can be used effectively by students following assignments prepared entirely by the teacher. The weaknesses that were identified in section A of this chapter can be overcome.

Weaknesses related to objectives

(The examples that follow describe an imaginary Road Safety course.)

A Road Safety text with interesting and informative statistics on road deaths before and after the introduction of compulsory seat belts may contain no specific learning objectives. These objectives can be incorporated easily as in the example below.

Assignment 10

Aim

At the end of this task you should be able to explain to others the effects seat belts had on the numbers of road accident victims.

Resources.

You will need Resource item **C** *"Road Accidents in Britain"*

Task

(1) Read Chapter 7 of *Road Accidents in Britain*

(2) Examine the statistics on road deaths before and after the introduction of seat belts

(3) What do the statistics show. Make some notes.

(4) Prepare a short, 3 - minute talk to the class explaining what you have discovered. Use evidence to prove your points.

The 'aims' for Assignment 10 are general - and this may suit this particular module. Teachers who read this assignment and say to themselves *I don't think much of that* will, with this approach, be able to reject it and redesign it to their own satisfaction.

There will be occasions when teachers might want to include on the assignment more specific objectives, and even details of attainment targets and assessment procedures.

The following example shows how this might be done:

> ## Assignment 11
>
> ### Aim
>
> At the end of this task you should be able to explain to others the effects of seat belts on the numbers of road accident victims
>
> ### Objectives
>
> (1) To be able to find, select and interpret data (AT4)
>
> (2) To be able to present information to an audience (AT7)
>
> ### Resources
>
> You will need resource item **C** *Road Accidents in Britain*
>
> ### Task
>
> etc...

If teachers create their own assignments the same resource can be used for different purposes:

> ## Assignment 12
>
> ### Aim
>
> Your aim is to present the statistics on road accidents in the form of a graph
>
> ### Resources.
>
> You will need resource item **C** *Road Accidents in Britain*
>
> ### Task
>
> 1. Read Chapter 7 of *Road Accidents in Britain*.
>
>   Prepare a line graph which shows...
> and so on...

Such assignments can easily be adapted to new ideas, syllabus requirements or technological changes.

For example, if the department concerned were able to provide access to a computer and associated software, the assignment could be adapted accordingly:

Assignment 13

Aim

Your aim is to produce a graph of accident statistics using the Gem Graph software programme etc.

Resources

You will need   (a) resource item **C** *Road Accidents in Britain*
                  (b) access to the computer

Task ...

Varied activities and assignments.

We have already seen variety in the section above on *objectives*.

Assignment 11....reading, writing, oral presentation

Assignment 12....reading, graphical presentation

Assignment 13....reading, use of IT

The same resource could also produce group work and role play:

Assignment 14

Aim

This is a group exercise. Your aim is to produce a short 'radio' discussion on the pros and cons of introducing compulsory seat belts.

Resources

You will need   (a) resource item **C** *Road Accidents in Britain*
                  (b) a cassette recorder and blank tape.

Task

(1) Each member of your group should read Chapters 6 and 7 of *Road Accidents in Britain*

(2) Each person should make notes on **key** points.

(3) Compare notes - did you all agree on what were the key points?

(4) List all the arguments for and against compulsory seat belts.

(5) Imagine your group is a panel brought together on radio to debate the subject. Decide who will speak **for** and who will speak **against** and who will 'chair' the discussion.

(6) Rehearse the debate and then record it.

You might want a more open-ended assignment involving problem-solving by a small group:

Assignment 15

Aim

This is a group task. Your task is to solve a problem that has worried the Police and Road Safety experts for many years: *How can we persuade young motorcyclists to wear bright, distinctive clothing?*

Resources

You will need   (a) resource item **C** *Road Accidents in Britain*
                  (b) the video *Mind How You Go*
                  (c) Resource items **F** - various motor cycle magazines
                  (d) your own experience

Task

Use any of the suggested resources.

(1) Do some research on the questions:
   - *What kinds of clothing do motor cyclists wear?*
   - *What problems are posed by some kinds of clothing?*

(2) Try to agree, in your group, a way in which young people can be persuaded to wear distinctive clothing.

(3) Prepare a ten-minute presentation using any evidence (video, photographs, props, illustrations) that you wish.

Using this approach teachers can provide regular opportunities for students to make use of the library or resource centre in more open-ended research:

Assignment 16

Aim

Your task is to undertake detailed research on one aspect of Road Safety which interests you.

Resources

You will need to make use of any resource you can find which helps you to find out more on your chosen topic.

Task

etc...

Any type of task can be set in this way, and, of course, a wide variety of resources can be introduced to supplement the core text *Road Accidents in Britain*. If the Librarian is involved in curriculum planning, then information on topics such as road safety can be collected in advance. (See Chapter 8 for more discussion on this issue.)

Cross-curricular themes

Issues such as Equal Opportunities, Health Education, Economic Awareness, Careers Guidance, may all be integrated successfully **at some point** in a course, theme or module:

Assignment 17

Aim

Your aim is to:

(1) research the cost of purchasing and running a second-hand car
(2) work out a monthly budget.

Resources

You will need:

(a) Resource item **H** *Which Car* magazine

(b) Resource item **Y** *Bank Loans*

(c) Resource item **Z** *Insurance details*

Task

(1) Read pages 16-18 of resource item **H** *Which Car* magazine. This article explains the pitfalls of buying secondhand cars.

(2) Study resource item Y....and so on...

The integration of such themes is best if it fits naturally with the topic you are studying. Forced integration rarely works and can produce resentment among staff and students. But opportunities will be there - and the creative and imaginative teacher will make full use of such opportunities.

Integration of adults and the community

Many schools and colleges have used adults and the community as valuable resources and here natural integration is so much more worthwhile.

The Road Safety Course provides ample opportunities to involve adults and agencies such as the Police, Motoring Organisations and Road Safety Officers. The links here are obvious.

Most curriculum areas will provide opportunities - less obvious perhaps, but they do exist. Once again the planning and creating of activities and assignments **separately** from the resources will allow teachers to expand their thinking and introduce students to the community and adults into the classroom at appropriate times.

Differentiation

Once you have established the principle of resources separated from assignments differentiation also becomes easier. Differentiation by task is resisted by some teachers who rightly fear the *self-fulfilling prophecy*.

This fear is well founded. Teachers who pre-determine the capability of students are in danger of setting those expectations in *concrete - **students achieve to the level expected of them and no more***. It is a familiar argument. This scenario is most closely associated with rigid forms of setting or streaming, and in classrooms where graded worksheets are used.

The ''A' worksheet is a rigid, inflexible tool and not all students will necessarily achieve to the same level in a wide range of activities and assignments. The same is true of the 'B' or 'C' worksheet.

If assignments are individually set, as in the assignments 11-17 illustrated earlier, greater flexibility is introduced. Some assignments will be *core* - undertaken by all students in a group. Some will be *enrichment* - undertaken by those who have quickly grasped basic concepts and who need to be extended. Some will be *reinforcement* - undertaken by those who have yet fully to grasp the basic understanding. A simple sequence of assignments may look like this.

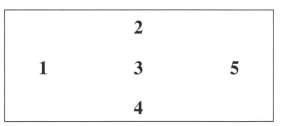

Tasks **1** and **5** are core.   Task **2** is a high level enrichment task.

Task **3** is lower level enrichment. Task **4** is a reinforcement task.

Tasks 2, 3 and 4 may differ either in (a) the resources they use, (b) the demands that are made, or (c) the kind of guidance that is given. For example:

Assignment 2 is open-ended and leaves the students to make decisions on resources, methods and forms of presentation:

Assignment 2

Aim

Your aim is to research the main causes of road accidents using as many sources of information as possible.

Resources

You will need resource items **A, B, J** and **L** and others you are able to find in the school or town library.

Task

1. Research the main causes of accidents

2. Present your findings in the most appropriate way

Assignment 3 provides more structure and advice:

Assignment 3

Aim

Your aim is to find out the main causes of road accidents.

Resources

You will need resource items **A B J** and **L**.

Task

(1) Read Chapter 7 in Resource Item **A**. Make notes on main points.

(2) Examine photographs in resource items **B** and **J**. Make notes.

(3) Read the newspaper article in resource item **L** - summarise main points.

(4) Write an essay entitled *The main causes of Road Accidents are.....*

In Assignment 4 more guidance is offered and the suggested headings provide models for students to follow:

Assignment 4

Aim

Your aim is to find out what causes road accidents

Resources

You will need resource items **B**, **J** and **L**.

Task

(1) Look at photographs in resources **B** and **J**. Write down what they show.

(2) Look at newspaper article in resource **L**

There are **4** main headings:

Safer Cars   Poor Driving   Laws   Drink & Driving

Under the 4 headings write as much as you can on how each can affect the number of road accidents

---

The decision on which of the available tasks might be followed will not be a 'fixed' decision based on apparent academic ability. The decision may be based on a number of factors:

- how well the student coped with the previous assignment
- how confident the student is feeling
- how well the student copes with open-ended assignments
- the reading level of the resources
- the degree to which the teacher wants to allow choice or negotiation
- the knowledge teachers have about students' needs in terms of guidance, models, structure etc.

Teachers may also be aware that students differ in their ability to handle instructional information.

The **DART** *(Directed Activities Related to Text)* strategy devised at Nottingham University recognises this and provides a series of activities designed to equip students to make full use of non-narrative texts.

Once again, the principle of DART can be integrated into a series of assignments. Students can learn how to use information by regular practice in the context of the subject or topic being studied.   Many English course books will also address this issue, *English Matters* by Cousins and Griffin (published by Stanley Thorne) being a good example.

The decision to *separate* activities and assignments allows the teacher, therefore, to:

- provide firmer objectives

- vary activities and assignments

- integrate, whenever possible, cross-curricular themes

- differentiate effectively.

This approach also provides greater flexibility in the teaching and learning approaches that can be used.

A six week *module* on road safety, for example, might see a teacher adopting a pattern such as:

Week 1	Introduction. Whole class. Video/visitor/discussion
Week 2	Independent assignments - core, enrichment or reinforcement
Week 3.	Group activity. Problem solving/role play
Week 4.	Group activity. Investigation/presentation/visit to community
Week 5.	Whole class. Groups report back/discussion
Week 6.	Independent work. Review, summary, assessment

The opportunities to integrate whole class teaching with small group, independent and active learning are enormous. This flexibility comes precisely because the teacher is **not** tied to the activities/assignments suggested in the resources being used.

Too often resources dictate to the teacher. This chapter has shown how teachers **should be** and **can be** in control.

Meeting the Needs

Network Educational Press will publish, in the Autumn, a handbook of In-Service Training workshops on meeting the needs of all students in mainstream classes. It will include guidance and workshop activities on:

- readability
- appropriate questioning
- differentiation of materials
- pictorial clues
- the special demands of the gifted student
- physical factors which have an influence on learning
- use of Information Technology
- recording and assessment.

The author, Cecilia Ferriman, is currently co-ordinator of Special Needs and Individualised Learning in a large comprehensive school. She has long experience of running workshops for staff and governors on meeting the needs of all students.

5

Study Guides

Types of Study Guide

Contexts for Study Guides

STUDY GUIDES

There are many situations which demand that students study
independently:

- ☐ the planning and execution of investigations or project work

- ☐ the 'negotiation' of learning routes or tasks

- ☐ the study of courses or modules where contact with a teacher or
  'tutor' is limited

- ☐ the planning and execution of group exercises

- ☐ the negotiation and completion of records of achievement

- ☐ the use of private study.

These demands appear at all levels of the educational system.

In the lower school working independently in the classroom can be
introduced regularly as was illustrated in the section on assignments in
Chapter 4. But as students grow older they will need to work
independently for longer periods.

This chapter examines ways in which study guides can be used to
support such independent work.

It begins in **Section A** by looking at different types of study guide:

- *open-ended* guides

- more tightly structured *(closed)* guides

- *semi-open, semi-closed* guides

- general *how to do* guides.

Section B examines a variety of contexts for using study guides:

- project work/coursework

- private study

- core skills

- careers guidance

- NVQ

- information/library skills

- supported self-study.

A   Types of study guide

Study guides take a variety of forms: they vary in length and scope, some are closed and others open-ended. Some contain a mixture of content, activity and assignments: others are merely guidance materials, directing students to content and activities stored elsewhere.

Despite their variety of forms, all good study guides provide the kind of support and guidance which students need when they are required to study independently. They can best be described by examining some examples.

An open-ended guide: Human Rights

The first example, on *Human Rights*, is an open-ended guide from the wide ranging *Network Educational Press* series (see page125). As you read through this guide (which is reduced from its original A4 size) make note of certain characteristics:

Page 1: It provides a clear title and specific aims and objectives

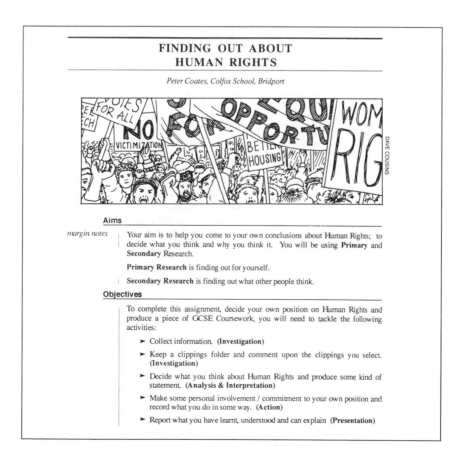

FINDING OUT ABOUT
HUMAN RIGHTS

Peter Coates, Colfox School, Bridport

Aims

margin notes   Your aim is to help you come to your own conclusions about Human Rights; to decide what you think and why you think it. You will be using **Primary** and **Secondary** Research.

Primary Research is finding out for yourself.

Secondary Research is finding out what other people think.

Objectives

To complete this assignment, decide your own position on Human Rights and produce a piece of GCSE Coursework, you will need to tackle the following activities:

► Collect information. **(Investigation)**

► Keep a clippings folder and comment upon the clippings you select. **(Investigation)**

► Decide what you think about Human Rights and produce some kind of statement. **(Analysis & Interpretation)**

► Make some personal involvement / commitment to your own position and record what you do in some way. **(Action)**

► Report what you have learnt, understood and can explain **(Presentation)**

Page 2: It provides advice on resources and other sources of information

Its layout allows students or teachers to add their own comments or notes

---

Coursework Enquiry Guide   Humanities : 16

Resources

margin notes

- AMNESTY INTERNATIONAL, 5 Robert's Place, off Bowling Green Lane, London EC1R OEJ
- NEW INTERNATIONALIST MAGAZINE, Freepost, Oxford OX1 2BC
- OXFAM EDUCATION DEPARTMENT, 274 Banbury Road, Oxford OX2 7DZ
- CHRISTIAN AID, Education Department, 240 Ferndale Road, London SW9 8BH
- HOWARD LEAGUE FOR PENAL REFORM, 320/322 Kennington Park Road, London SE11 4PP
- ACTION AID, Hamlyn House, Archway, London N19 5PG
- THE UNITED NATIONS INFORMATION CENTRE, 14-15 Stratford Place, London W1N 9AF

- ANTI-SLAVERY SOCIETY, 180 Brixton Road London SW9 6AT
- THE COUNCIL FOR EDUCATION IN WORLD CITIZENSHIP, Seymour Mews House, Seymour Mews, London W1H 9PE
- BRITISH COUNCIL OF CHURCHES, Human Rights Advisory Forum, 2 Eaton Gate, London SW1W 9BL
- THE CENTRE FOR GLOBAL EDUCATION, University of York, York YO1 5DD
- ANTI-APARTHEID MOVEMENT, 13 Selous Street, London NW1 0DW
- DEVELOPMENT EDUCATION CENTRE, Selly Oak College, Bristol Road, Birmingham B29 6LE
- COUNCIL OF EUROPE, Human Rights Division, 67006 Strasbourg, CEDEX, France

Activities

Activity 1

Collect as many resources as you can from the organisations listed above, writing or telephoning where necessary. Explain what you are doing and what kind of information you require Try your school and local libraries. Geography, RE and English Teachers may also be able to help with resources including videos on the subject. Keep all of the information that you receive safely, you will need to use it and it will form part of your final report.

Activity 2 : Deciding what you think

While you are waiting for all the information to arrive (some of it may take some time) you can begin to decide what you really think about Human Rights. Sounds good - you believe in it - but what does it mean?

In Britain and most of the countries in the NORTH, we associate 'Rights' with personal freedom, political or religious beliefs. To someone starving in one of the countries in the Southern Hemisphere, and lacking medical treatment, sanitation and education - our view of 'Rights' may sound like a luxury.

To start this sort of serious thinking you need to begin with yourself and then spread outwards. Begin by asking yourself the following questions and noting down your answers.

- What are my own rights?
- What are my friends rights?
- What are the rights of my family?
- What are the rights of the Police?

- What are the rights of the Media?
- What are the rights of the Trade Unions?
- What are the rights of Government?

---

page 2   *NEP Guides also in Geography & Business Studies*

Page 3: The suggested activities are open-ended and in no way prescribed
Ideas and stimulus are offered at all stages

Coursework Enquiry Guide   Humanities : 16

margin notes Talk over your ideas with your teacher, with your friends and with someone who disagrees with you; then go on to consider these questions:

- Are rights the same as responsibilities?
- Can different rights cause conflict?
- Have governments the rights to ignore rights?

When you have considered all of these questions sum up your feelings either through writing, artwork, music, drama or by making an audio-visual record. You may like to arrange a formal debate about a Rights issue or invite a visiting speaker into your school to give a talk and answer questions. Whatever you decide to do, keep a record.

Note - Some GCSE Humanities syllabuses will accredit these kinds of non-written contribution as coursework - check with your teacher.

Activity 3 : Keep a Clippings File

Over a period of a few weeks keep a clippings file of newspaper / periodical articles on all kinds of Human Rights issues. Add your own comments to the articles which you collect. If you don't have a paper at home and can't afford to buy one, ask your teacher or school librarian to help. The completed file will form part of your final report.

Activity 4 : Getting involved

Are you prepared to get involved and commit yourself to your beliefs? In Britain we enjoy a wide variety of Human Rights, but this has not always been the case. Many of the rights and freedoms which we enjoy (and that includes being at school) were hard won over a long period by people of whom you will never hear anything. Not everyone in Britain enjoys all the rights set out by the United Nations. Elsewhere in the world some have few rights at all. Do you care enough to do something positive? If you do here are some suggestions:

- Try to start a Young Amnesty group in your school.
- See if you can persuade you form to adopt a child for Action Aid. It costs £10.00 a month, (in a class of 30 it would cost each person approx 35p).
- Arrange to work in a charity shop on a Saturday for a few weeks.
- Arrange a sponsored event.
- Arrange a jumble sale.

Keep a **full diary** of what you do - it will form part of your final report.

Activity 5 : Presentation

This final activity involves you in making a report. You should already have acquired:

- published material *(Activity 1)*
- your own statement *(Activity 2)*
- a clippings file *(Activity 3)*
- a diary *(Activity 4)*

© *Network Educational Press*   *page 3*

Page 4: Advice and support is provided on general approaches and on methods of presentation

margin notes

By now you should have a clear idea of what Human Rights means to you and others. You may have developed your own personal list of *'Rights' priorities* and be working towards their realisation. At the very least you should have understood that Human Rights affects *everyone everywhere*.

How you present your **final report** will be up to you, your teacher and in part be determined by the syllabus you are following. Here are some ideas to consider:

➤ Present everything which you completed in **Activities 1 to 4** in a file. Add an introduction and a conclusion. Large documents might be included as an Appendix.

➤ Arrange a **wall display** of your work.

➤ Take a **lesson** on Human Rights with your class.

➤ Take an **assembly** on Human Rights.

➤ If you did some drama, artwork or music for **Activity 2,** you may like to present it to a wider audience as part of a Human Rights event which you could organise in school for a lunchtime or after school.

Presentation : General Hints

However you decide to present your Final Report, you need to make it as informative and interesting as you can.

➤ Aim to maintain interest by variety - this applies whether your presentation is spoken or written.

➤ Use visual aids - newspapers, photographs, diagrams, maps, video presentations - all make a report more interesting.

➤ Label all newspaper cuttings, diagrams, maps carefully and say where they came from.

➤ Remember to include any suggestions for further work that you might have done given the time.

➤ Describe ways in which you might have improved your study and note any problems you faced when completing the coursework.

If you have chosen a written report, **number all pages** and make out a **Contents Page** to put in at the beginning of your report, immediately after your Title Page.

Finally, put in a written 'thank you' *(acknowledgement)* to all the people and organisations who helped you to carry out your investigation.

Go back and check your work - **Be neat, Be careful, Be organised !**

> **The Task in Brief**
>
> Find out about Human Rights
>
> Decide what you think
>
> Collect information
>
> Get involved
>
> Report

A 'closed' study guide

The second example, *Traffic Flow Survey*, is more highly structured.

This kind of study guide is invaluable where a teacher wants an individual or group to have the confidence to work independently, but where 'choice' is not an issue. (Students may well, of course, have 'chosen' to do a traffic study in the first place).

Page 1: The aims of the investigation are explained in simple, student-friendly language

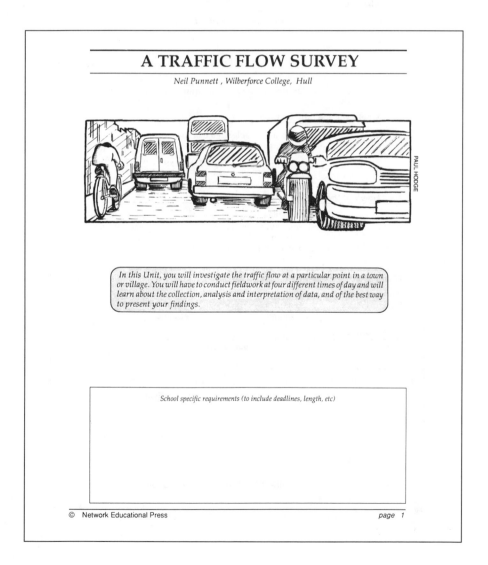

A TRAFFIC FLOW SURVEY

Neil Punnett , Wilberforce College, Hull

PAUL HODGE

In this Unit, you will investigate the traffic flow at a particular point in a town or village. You will have to conduct fieldwork at four different times of day and will learn about the collection, analysis and interpretation of data, and of the best way to present your findings.

School specific requirements (to include deadlines, length, etc)

© Network Educational Press   *page 1*

Page 2: Clear, practical advice on procedures to be followed.
          Models of how to record data

Coursework Enquiry Guide   Geography : 8

AIM   To investigate

Margin notes   "*The factors influencing traffic flow through the day at a particular*
                      point in a town or village"

Data needed

You will need to collect information on traffic flows, direction and
pattern.

It will be best to collect this information at four chosen times on one
day.

Where will the data be found

- Choose a suitable stretch of road for study. It should be a busy
  road running into the centre of the town or village.

- Do not choose a junction unless you have some friends to help
  you because you will find it very difficult to handle all the
  traffic on your own.

How will the data be collected

- Read the sections in the textbooks listed above under **Resources
  and Equipment**. Each includes a specimen of the traffic survey
  table you will need in the field. Make a copy of one of them, or
  use the example given below:

TRAFFIC SURVEY SHEET (GCSE COURSEWORK) _____SCHOOL									
Name of Pupil:_____ **Date of Survey:** ___/___/___									
TIME FROM:_____(am/pm) **LOCATION: Grid Ref**_____ or									
TO:_____(am/pm) **Street/Junc**_____									
Weather Conditions:_____									
CARS		LORRIES/BUSES/ TRACTORS ETC		MOTORCYCLES		BICYCLES		OTHER VEHICLES	
TO	FROM	TO	FROM	TO	FROM	TO	FROM	TO	FROM
		(To/From Town Centres - or travelling North/South)							

Table 1 (T1) Traffic Survey Sheet

© Network Educational Press

Page 3: More models and general safety advice.
The remaining pages follow a similar pattern

Coursework Enquiry Guide   Geography : 8

Margin notes

- Sort out clearly what you intend to do. Conducting a traffic survey properly is a tiring task because it requires constant concentration. It is best to conduct the survey for a period of no more than thirty minutes. For a very busy road fifteen minutes will do.

- Choose four times of day to carry out your census. Ideally you should aim for the busy periods in the morning and afternoon (say 8.30 a.m. and 5.00 p.m.) and two other times.

BE CAREFUL

When you arrive at the stretch of road you are going to survey make sure that you find a safe place to carry out the census. It should be:

- **SAFE FOR YOU** - well away from the kerbside,
- **SAFE FOR PEDESTRIANS** - not blocking the pavement
- **SAFE FOR ROAD USERS** - not blocking their view.

- When you have selected a safe position make a careful note of the time of starting your census. Record the traffic passing in both directions by using a tally count such as that below:

CARS		LORRIES/BUSES/ TRACTORS ETC		MOTORCYCLES		BICYCLES		OTHER VEHICLES	
TO	FROM	TO	FROM	TO	FROM	TO	FROM	TO	FROM
		(To/From Town Centres - or travelling North/South)							

Table 2 (T2) Tally Count

- At the end of the survey period write the time on your census sheet and count up the total numbers of vehicles.

Resources and Equipment

You will find the following resources and equipment useful. Your teacher should be able to advise you on whether they are available in school, and your school library or local library will almost certainly be able to help you.

© Network Educational Press   *page 3*

Semi-open, semi-closed guides

It is very easy to prepare guides which provide both structured, fairly prescriptive guidance **and** opportunities for open-ended study.

The third example, *The European Community - 1992*, does just that.

Page 1: A general summary and specific aims clearly set out

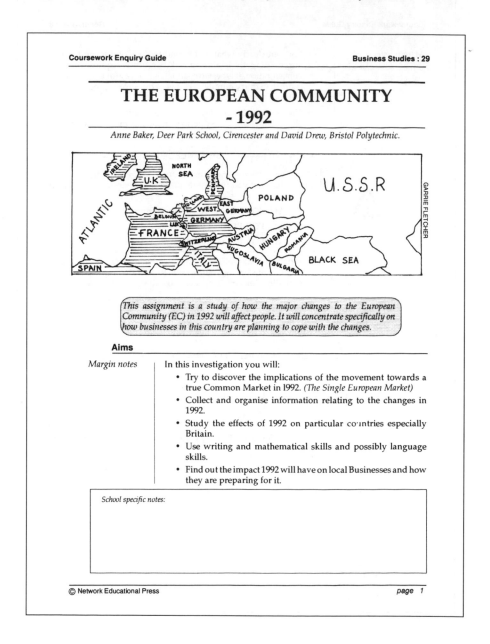

Coursework Enquiry Guide   Business Studies : 29

THE EUROPEAN COMMUNITY
- 1992

Anne Baker, Deer Park School, Cirencester and David Drew, Bristol Polytechnic.

This assignment is a study of how the major changes to the European Community (EC) in 1992 will affect people. It will concentrate specifically on how businesses in this country are planning to cope with the changes.

Aims

Margin notes

In this investigation you will:

- Try to discover the implications of the movement towards a true Common Market in 1992. *(The Single European Market)*
- Collect and organise information relating to the changes in 1992.
- Study the effects of 1992 on particular countries especially Britain.
- Use writing and mathematical skills and possibly language skills.
- Find out the impact 1992 will have on local Businesses and how they are preparing for it.

School specific notes:

© Network Educational Press   *page 1*

Page 2: *Extensive guidance on relevant resources and sources of information*

Coursework Enquiry Guide   **Business Studies : 29**

Resources

Margin notes

The following organisations will provide information on the subject.

- **Department of Trade and Industry** - (write to the Industry/Education Unit, DTI, *Ashdown House, 123 Victoria Street, London SW1E 6RB*)
- **EC Commission** (British Office of the EC, *20 Kensington Gardens, London.*
- **Understanding British Industry** (*Sun Alliance House, New Inn Hall Street, Oxford OX1 2QE.*)
- **Understanding Industry** (*91 Waterloo Road, London SE1 8XP*)
- **Trades Union Congress** (*Congress House, Great Russell Street, London WC1B 3LS*)

In addition you may want to write to the local office of your **MEP** (European Member of Parliament)

- Newspapers and magazines are a valuable source of information particularly:
  - **The Economist**
  - **The Investor**
  - The financial pages of the 'serious' newspapers (*Guardian, Times, Telegraph* and *Independent*)
  - The Sunday supplements - which may run features.
- Television and Radio may run special programmes on the subject - watch the Radio and TV Times for details.
- Commercial Videos have been published on the subject - look out for advertisements in the serious newspapers.
- **Prestel, TTNS, NERIS** (via **Campus 2000**) will have up-to-date information.
- Your text books will have a section on 1992.

Additional resources suggested by your Teacher

© Network Educational Press

Page 3: Closed and open activities offered.
      The remaining pages of the guide follow a similar pattern

---

Coursework Enquiry Guide   **Business Studies : 29**

Activities

Margin notes

Introduction

The changes to the European Community in 1992 is a vast subject.
The activities below provide a range of possible investigations.
The structure below may help in the planning.

ACTIVITY STRUCTURE FOR '1992'		Optional/ Recommeded
Activity 1	Brainstorming/ Listing what is already known	Recommended
Activity 2	Research EC1992	Recommended
Activity 3	Analysing Research	Recommended
Activity 4	Survey of Community Knowledge	Optional
Activity 5	Survey of Local Business Plans for 1992	Optional
Activity 6	Debate/Discussion involving Community	Optional
Activity 7	Exchange of Information via Twinning Town	Optional
Activity 8	Video Presentation	Optional

Activity 1

This activity can be done individually or as part of a small group.
Make a list *(or hold a brainstorming session if part of a group)* of what you
already know about 1992.

Do not worry about the phrasing or wording of your list - just put the
ideas down on paper.

Once you have done this, try to sort your ideas under headings.
(Employment, trade, Cultural etc.)

Activity 2

Collect as much information as you can on each of the headings you
decided on in *Activity 1.*

Use the sources listed in the Resources section.

If you write to organisations or people, explain what you are doing
and what it is you want to know.

"Please send me information on EC 1992" is not enough. **Highlight.
Be specific.**

E.g.

*"I am interested in finding out more about the laws on employment
across the European Community."*

When you write, be sure to enclose a large stamped, self-addressed
envelope.

© Network Educational Press   *page 3*

The general *how to do* study guide

Some study guides will be general in nature. They can be used to give general advice and guidance on course content, methods of working, assessment procedures and so on.

The 'how to do' study guide can be useful in all kinds of situations where students need guidance but where the individual attention of the teacher is unnecessary and inappropriate.

The fourth example is *Preparing for Questionnaires and Interviews: the kind of guide which might be used in a variety of contexts.*

Page 1: General aims clearly expressed

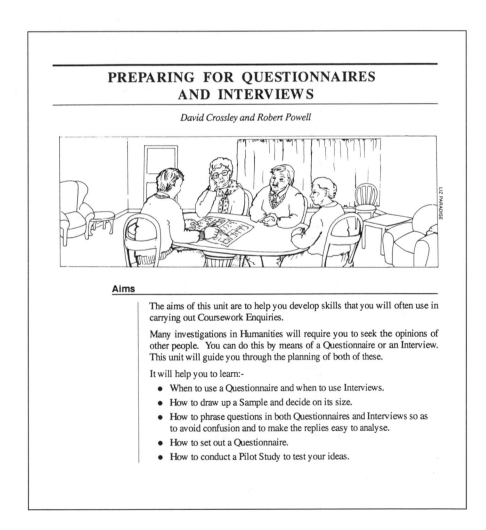

PREPARING FOR QUESTIONNAIRES AND INTERVIEWS

David Crossley and Robert Powell

Aims

The aims of this unit are to help you develop skills that you will often use in carrying out Coursework Enquiries.

Many investigations in Humanities will require you to seek the opinions of other people. You can do this by means of a Questionnaire or an Interview. This unit will guide you through the planning of both of these.

It will help you to learn:-

- When to use a Questionnaire and when to use Interviews.
- How to draw up a Sample and decide on its size.
- How to phrase questions in both Questionnaires and Interviews so as to avoid confusion and to make the replies easy to analyse.
- How to set out a Questionnaire.
- How to conduct a Pilot Study to test your ideas.

Page 2: Introduction to key concepts

COURSEWORK ENQUIRY GUIDE

Questionnaire or Interview?

The first thing you will have to decide is whether to use a questionnaire, interview, or a combination of both.

A **questionnaire** usually requires short answers, is fairly simple to administer and can be given to fairly large numbers of people. **Interviews** provide longer, more detailed answers, but take longer, and cannot involve too many people.

You might like to consider a combination of both - a questionnaire to provide a wide range of responses and one or two interviews to put some feeling into a topic. Questionnaire results alone are often dull sets of statistics.

Samples

You now need to decide who you are going to question. You cannot normally ask everyone who may have opinions on a topic, so you have to choose a small number. The group you choose to question is called a *sample*.

How large a Sample?

- Too small a sample will not give you enough information.
- Too large a sample will take too long.

So be realistic and think carefully about the time available before you choose the size of your sample.

Random or structured sample?

A *random* sample - eg. every fourth pupil in a class list - may suit some investigations, but be careful if attempting this with members of the public. Talk to your teacher first.

A *structured* sample, however, may be necessary in other investigations where you want to choose a representative group.

For example, if you wanted to do some research in your school, a sample of **10%** would look like this:

School	Number	Sample
Total	1,000	100
Boys	500	50
Girls	500	50
Each Year-Group	200	20

A structured sample is not easy to organise, and you may need to ask your teacher for help. It would be easier simply to ask your friends to fill in questionnaires but the results would not necessarily be representative of the school as a whole.

In the same way, an Enquiry in the community is easy if you simply ask all your friends, relatives and neighbours. You may need a more structured and representative sample, with a cross-section of the population. Ask your teacher for advice on this.

Page 3: Real examples to help students understand issues

If you are unable to choose exactly the right sample for your Enquiry, do not worry, **but remember to point this out in your final report.**

Questionnaires

Devising Questions

Some questions are easy to give a Yes or No answer to.

"Do you ever listen to Pop Music?" *Yes* ☐ *No* ☐

Others need more options.

"Do you like Pop Music?" *All kinds* ☐ *Some* ☐ *None* ☐

Avoid bad questions like:

"What kind of Pop Music do you like?"

This kind of question will produce many different kinds of answer and will be difficult to analyse. It is better to ask the question like this:

"Which kinds of Pop Music do you like?"

Rock ☐	Soul ☐	Heavy Metal ☐	Rap ☐
Reggae ☐	Ballads ☐	House ☐	*Tick one or more.*
Disco ☐	New Beat ☐	Other ☐	

Leading Questions

It is possible to phrase questions that make it clear what answer you want. For example:

"In fox-hunting, do you think it is awful that defenceless foxes are torn apart by a pack of hounds?"

This question is designed in such a way that the person being questioned feels compelled to answer *'Yes'*.

Try to avoid this mistake - Examiners will not give you credit for biased, leading questions

'Double' Questions

"Do you think that smoking and drinking ought to be banned in public places?"   Yes ☐   No ☐

What about the person who thinks that smoking ought to be banned, but not drinking?

Avoid 'double' questions like this.

Ambiguous questions

Sometimes you can ask questions which are ambiguous. For example: in a study of democratic rights you might ask a question:

Page 5: Visual models again provide students with practical ideas.
The remaining pages in this guide follow a similar pattern

COURSEWORK ENQUIRY GUIDE

Layout of Questionnaire

If your questionnaire asks people to tick from a selection of boxes, it is a good idea to put the boxes on the right-hand edge of the paper. When your questionnaires are returned you can then lay them out slightly overlapping, so that you can easily count up all the ticks for any one box.
(see diagram **Q1** below)

EXAMPLE QUESTIONNAIRE (Q1) POP MUSIC

Do you ever listen to pop music?	Yes	☐
	No	☐
Do you like Pop music?	All kinds	☐
	Some	☐
	None	☐
Which kinds of Pop Music do you like?	Tick 1 or more	
	Rock	☐
	Soul	☐
	Heavy Metal	☐
	Rap	☐
	Reggae	☐
	Ballads	☐
	House	☐
	Disco	☐
	New Beat	☐
	Other	☐

If you have access to a computer, you may be able to code the replies in such a way that all kinds of analyses can be done. Ask your teacher for advice on this but remember if you are using a computer it is even more important to use boxes along the right hand edge, to enable you to input the data easily and accurately.

Study guides, therefore, can vary in the degree to which they allow student choice.

The three illustrated were all part of the *Network Educational Press* series but other publishers produce study guides of a different type. Many of the distance learning or open learning courses use study guides to help students structure their time and work.

The *National Extension College*, for example, publishes a wide range of courses for the independent learner and some of its study guides are like books themselves - a mixture of information, stimulus, guidance and self assessments.

The *Wessex Project* in the South West has produced a wide range of 'A' level study guides.   These guides tend to be self contained and provide some content as well as activities, assignments and self assessment questions.

Such guides provide solid support to the independent learner but in some respects lack the flexibility of the short format approach.

Flexibility is required in a variety of contexts and these are explored in more detail in section B.

B Contexts for Study Guides

Project work/coursework

Study guides can be used to support project work/coursework in a number of ways:

- few teachers will want students to choose the same coursework projects - a range of short format guides will provide choice

- the range will also allow teachers to differentiate and to provide opportunities for both open-ended and closed activities/assignments

- the short format guide can easily be updated/reviewed in the light of new developments or resources or as a result of evaluation

- the short format guide will allow teachers to offer a range of *different* activities which nevertheless make use of the *same* collection of resources.

Private study

If you ask a group of post-16 students or their teachers how well private study time is used you will rarely receive a positive response. In most institutions it is used badly. The imaginative use of study guides would almost certainly improve the situation.

A small group of 'A' level students might, for example, be given the task of researching a particular concept, idea, character or event. A study guide would provide a set of guidelines, providing advice on resources, questions, and ways of presenting findings. The expectation would be set that each group would report back in a *seminar* to the teacher and the rest of the class. This structured assignment would improve the use of private study and, with the help of the study guide, students would develop the skills of both research and presentation, and their communication skills would be enhanced.

Core skills post-16

Those debating how to implement core skills post-16 might usefully adopt study guides as a means of developing communication, numeracy etc. in the context of the subjects being studied. Where non-specialists (e.g. tutors) are being asked to deliver core skills (e.g. Modern Languages) outside their own specialism, then study guides written in collaboration with specialists might provide them with valuable support.

Careers guidance

Many schools struggle to provide careers guidance through the tutorial system. Form tutors take on this responsibility, many with great enthusiasm, but they often lack the confidence or the specialist knowledge to counsel effectively.

Careers libraries are often badly used. Students generally cannot find their way through the maze of literature/videos that exist and the resulting interviews or tutorials are often uninformed and 'general'. The production of a range of study guides ranging from the *general* to the *specific* would transform the situation.

Tutors could discuss in broad terms the career choices of students. The students could use the study guides to direct them to specific resources, and to address certain issues and questions. The follow-up tutorial would then be much more valuable: the student would have done some research and the tutor would be able to use the study guide as the agenda.

The preparation of study guides for careers could be taken on by teams of careers specialists, tutors and local employers - a useful and practical way to involve industry and education.

National Vocational Qualifications (NVQ)

Once the NVQ proposals are fully implemented teachers in FE will face the prospect of teaching groups with widely differing levels of competence. Their learning needs will be different and an 'open learning' pack for each is unrealistic.

A series of study guides would allow teachers to identify different entry points and to set assignments and activities specific to the needs of individuals.

The *same* set of resources - texts, videos, software etc., might be used for *different* purposes by *different* students. The study guide gives teachers that flexibility.

Information skills

Chapter 7, *Managing Resources* argues strongly for the close involvement of the librarian and resource centre manager in curriculum planning.

If students are to develop the skills of finding, selecting and using information of all kinds they need to have regular practice. The one-off library lesson or occasional use of a computer database is unlikely to develop such skills. Teachers need to integrate the use of libraries with their normal teaching and study guides planned in conjunction with the librarian can play a major role in this (see Chapter 8).

Supported self-study

Supported self-study is used in many schools as a method of developing independent skills and student autonomy. Students work independently for varying periods receiving regular support from a teacher or 'tutor'.

Many students follow examination courses - often in what are termed 'minority' subjects - where their contact with a tutor is minimal. The study guide can be enormously helpful in both situations. Students can find supported self-study difficult to cope with - the loneliness and self- discipline of working alone can cause problems and a well designed study guide can provide invaluable support.

The supported self-study tutorial can also be considerably enhanced by the use of study guides. They provide a *focus,* an *agenda* for discussion and planning and, if the format allows, notes can be made on the study guide itself as a result of the negotiations that take place. 'Ownership' of the assignment is more readily assured. (See illustration overleaf.)

The example below is taken from an imaginary small-group tutorial where students and teacher are planning an investigation on pollution - the study guide forms part of the agenda. The students have been encouraged to make notes and to include any agreements that are made between students and teacher or between students themselves.

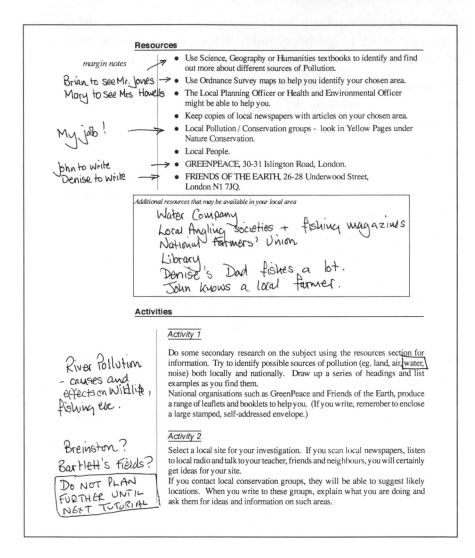

Study guides, therefore, can be used in a wide range of contexts.

Two major concerns need to be aired, however: the design of such guides and the time to prepare them.

Design is examined in the next Chapter and *Time* in Chapter 8.

The Layout and Design
of Learning Materials

Layout and Design

Desktop Publishing

THE LAYOUT AND DESIGN OF LEARNING MATERIALS

This book has argued strongly that teachers should not spend long hours developing their own materials. The creation of good assignments and study guides provide greater flexibility, but the *content* of such guides is only one consideration.

The assignment or study guide must look *attractive* and be easily *accessible* to the user. This chapter looks at simple rules and techniques for improving the layout and design of documents and examines the potential of desktop publishing.

The advice that is offered applies generally to materials that are produced within an institution. There are, therefore, examples of documents other than study guides and assignments.

The chapter has two main sections:

(A) Layout and design, and (B) Desktop publishing

 Layout and Design

This section will look at layout and design under the following headings:

- ☐ Aims and objectives
- ☐ Language
- ☐ Structure/headings
- ☐ Layout
- ☐ Emphasis
- ☐ Graphics/illustrations

Aims and objectives

The case for clearly defined aims and objectives was examined in Chapter 4 - students invariably benefit if they can see *why* they are undertaking a particular assignment, *where* it is leading and *how* they will be assessed.

A study guide ought, therefore, to explain clearly what the aims and objectives are. There are a variety of ways of doing this and examples follow.

This example is ***Traffic Study***, unit no. 31 in the *Network Educational Press **Geography*** series.

The aims of the study are expressed in straightforward, student-friendly language

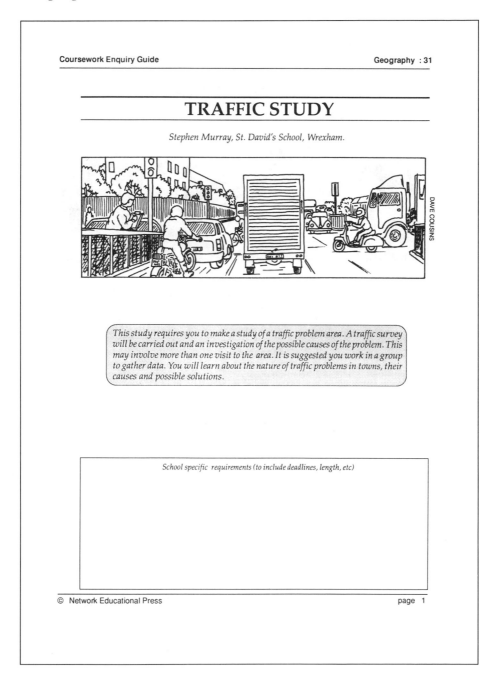

This example is *A Share in the Market*, unit no. 5 in the *Network Educational Press Business Studies* series.

A general introduction with more formal aims

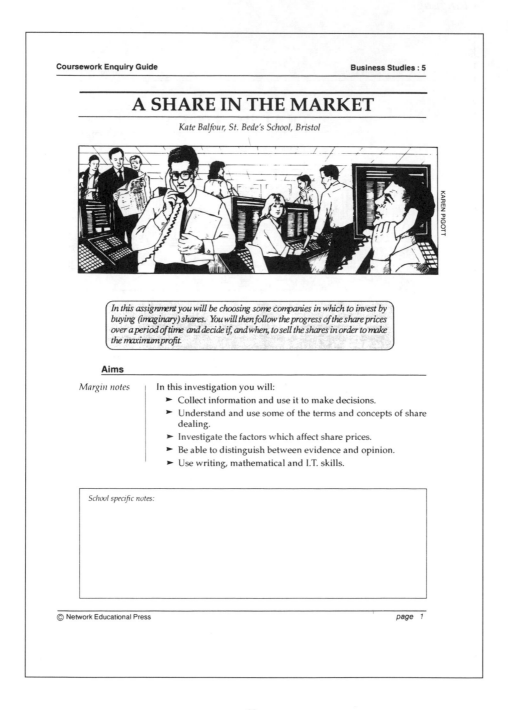

This example is ***Planning provisions for the Elderly in a Local Community***, unit no. 18 in the *Network Educational Press **Humanities** series.*

More exam-oriented language including 'technical' terms

PLANNING PROVISIONS FOR THE ELDERLY IN A LOCAL COMMUNITY

Sue Hallam, Pen Park School, Bristol

Aims

margin notes

Your aim is to identify existing provisions for the elderly and to suggest what **new** provisions should be established. You will need to investigate and understand the needs of the elderly, and what is lacking.

You will be using **Primary research** - finding out for yourself, and **Secondary research** - finding out what other people think.

Objectives

To complete this assignment you will need to:

➤ Collect information on existing provisions in your local community. **(Investigation)**

➤ Interview local elderly people to find out what they think their needs are. **(Investigation)**

➤ Present a reasoned explanation of your views and findings. **(Presentation)**

School specific requirements (deadline, length, etc)

Language

The language used in a study guide must obviously match the target user, and if it is too advanced or too 'simple' students might be negative towards the guide from the beginning. It is a good idea to make the language concise, straightforward and 'friendly' - conversational rather than academic. Do not patronise, however.

Guides that are too wordy will produce an adverse reaction. If a document like the one below were put in a teacher's pigeon hole it would be 'filed' instantly!

Assessing The Role Of Conservation In An Urban Area

Your aim is to examine the role of Conservation Policy in an urban area. The first thing that you need to do is to choose an area to study. Once you have done this you will then need to find out what the conservation policy is for this area,if any, how effective it has been, and why it was necessary to have one in the first place.

You will have to use a variety of methods, but the main method will be Primary research. This is a method where you will collect information for yourself from your chosen area.

You will have to carry out a number of important activities.

The first thing you will have to do is to find an area or building(s) that have been conserved. All this early part of your work is called Investigation. Your task is to find out as much as you possibly can about the site through a fieldwork visit.

You will then have to do some more investigations and find out about the site from sources such as libraries. Your next task is to design a questionnaire so that you will be able to go out and find out what local people's opinions are about the site.

When you have done this you will have to undertake the important task of evaluating your findings which involves you in what is called analysis. Next you will have to look carefully at what you have done and draw conclusions from your findings. This part of the work is called interpretation.

Finally you will have to decide how you are going to report what you have learned to other people. This part of the study is called presentation.

Structure and Headings

All documents will benefit from a clear and consistent structure. Major headings, sub-headings, minor headings should follow a pattern. The headings should allow students to find their way round the document, and if lengthy, a regular summary of key points will help. The wordy extract from the previous page is transformed (a) by editing and (b) by introducing a series of bold headings and sub-headings.

*(a) The wordy extract from the previous page is first **EDITED**:*

ASSESSING THE ROLE OF
CONSERVATION IN AN URBAN AREA

Aims

Your aim is to examine the role of Conservation Policy on an urban area. You will need to choose an area to study. You will then need to find out what the conservation policy is, how effective it has been, and why it was necessary.

The main method you will use is primary research where you will collect information for yourself from your chosen area.

Objectives

These are the things that you have to do:

find an area or building(s) that have been conserved. (Investigation)

investigate and find out about the site through a fieldwork visit. (Investigation)

investigate and find out about the site from sources in libraries. (Investigation)

design a questionnaire to find out what local people's opinions are about the site. (Investigation)

evaluate your findings. (Analysis)

draw conclusions from your findings. (Interpretation)

report what you have learned to other people. (Presentation)

---

and (b) **IMPROVED** *with headings and sub-headings:*

ASSESSING THE ROLE OF CONSERVATION IN AN URBAN AREA

Aims

Your aim is to examine the role of Conservation Policy on an urban area. You will need to choose an area to study. You will then need to find out what the conservation policy is, how effective it has been and why it was necessary.

The main method you will use is primary research, where you will collect information for yourself from your chosen area.

Objectives

These are the things that you have to do:

find an area or building(s) that have been conserved. (Investigation)

investigate and find out about the site through a fieldwork visit. (Investigation)

investigate and find out about the site from sources in libraries. (Investigation)

design a questionnaire to find out what local people's opinions are about the site. (Investigation)

evaluate your findings. (Analysis)

draw conclusions from your findings. (Interpretation)

report what you have learned to other people. (Presentation)

---

and (c) **COMPLETED** *with an illustration and a few design features including emphasis*

ASSESSING THE ROLE OF
CONSERVATION IN AN URBAN AREA

Mandy Boyle, Pen Park School, Bristol

Aims

margin notes

Your aim is to examine the role of Conservation Policy on an **Urban area.** You will need to choose an area to study. You will then need to find out what conservation policy is, how effective it has been, and why it was necessary.

The main method you will use is **Primary research,** where you will collect information for yourself from your chosen area.

Objectives

These are the things that you have to do:

➤ Find an area or building(s) that have been conserved. **(Investigation)**

➤ Investigate and find out about the site through a fieldwork visit. **(Investigation)**

➤ Investigate and find out about the site from sources in libraries. **(Investigation)**

➤ Design a questionnaire to find out what local people's opinions are about the site. **(Investigation)**

➤ Evaluate your findings. **(Analysis)**

➤ Draw conclusions from your findings. **(Interpretation)**

➤ Report what you have learned to other people. **(Presentation)**

School specific requirements (deadline, length etc)

---

page 1

Layout

The overall effect of a document has much to do with design and layout.

The examples that follow are taken from *Looking Good in Print* by Roger C Parker and published by Ventana Press (ISBN 0-940087-05-7). This publication is, in our opinion, the best available book on document design, and we are grateful to the publisher for allowing us to use extracts from it.

Columns

Columns can often make a document more accessible. The flyer below is uninviting

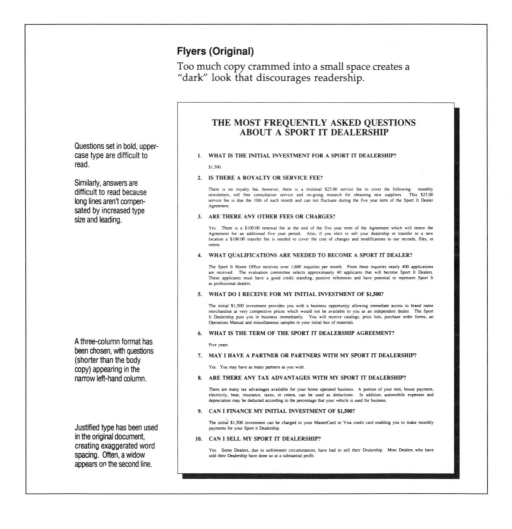

The same document redesigned to make use of columns makes it more accessible

Design Makeovers

Flyers (Makeover)

A staggered three-column format clearly separates questions and answers, allowing the reader to pick and choose specific areas of interest.

A "friendlier" typeface has been chosen, set ragged right.

Shorter lines and narrower columns make the answers more readable.

SPORT IT

The Most Frequently Asked Questions About A Sport It Dealership

1. **Is there a royalty or service fee?**

There is no royalty fee, however, there is a minimal $25.00 service fee to cover the following: monthly newsletters, toll free consultation service and on-going research for obtaining new suppliers. This $25.00 service fee is due the 10th of each month and can not fluctuate during the five year term of the Sport It Dealer Agreement.

2. **What is the initial investment for a Sport It Dealership?**

$1,500.

3. **Are there any other fees?**

Yes. There is a $100.00 renewal fee at the end of the five year term of the Agreement which will renew the Agreement for an additional five year period. Also, if you elect to sell your dealership or transfer to a new location a $100.00 transfer fee is needed to cover the cost of changes and modifications to our records, files, et cetera.

4. **What qualifications are needed to become a Sport It Dealer?**

The Sport It Home Office receives over 1,600 inquiries per month. From these inquiries nearly 400 applications are received. The evaluation committee selects approximately 40 applicants that will become Sport It Dealers. These applicants must have a good credit standing, positive references and have potential to represent Sport It as professional dealers.

5. **What do I receive for my initial investment of $1,500?**

The initial $1,500 investment provides you with a business opportunity allowing immediate access to brand name merchandise at very competitive prices which would not be available to you as an independent dealer. The Sport It Dealership puts you in business immediately. You will receive catalogs, prices lists, purchase order forms, Operations Manual and miscellaneous sample merchandise in your initial box of materials.

6. **What is the term of the Sport It Dealership Agreement?**

Five years.

7. **May I have a partner or partners with my Sport It Dealership?**

Yes. You may have as many partners as you wish.

8. **Are there any tax advantages with my Sport It Dealership?**

There are many tax advantages available for your home operated business. A portion of your rent, house payment, electricity, heat, insurance, taxes, et cetera can be used as deductions. In addition, automobile expenses and depreciation may be deducted according to the percentage that your vehicle is used for business.

9. **Can I finance my initial investment of $1,500?**

The initial $1,500 investment can be charged to your MasterCard or Visa credit card enabling you to make monthly payments for your Sport It Dealership.

Emphasis

Certain important messages can be emphasised by the use of bold, italics, type size, screens or boxes. Contrast the two versions of this newsletter
Version 1

Putting Your Knowledge to Work

Newsletters (Original)

This piece demonstrates how design principles applied inappropriately can result in a poorly designed document.

The rules in the body copy tend to fight with the illustration box and rules in the masthead.

Nonproportional typefaces create uneven word spacing.

Indention within narrow columns often causes awkward blocks of white space.

Version 2 *of this document is transformed from the original*

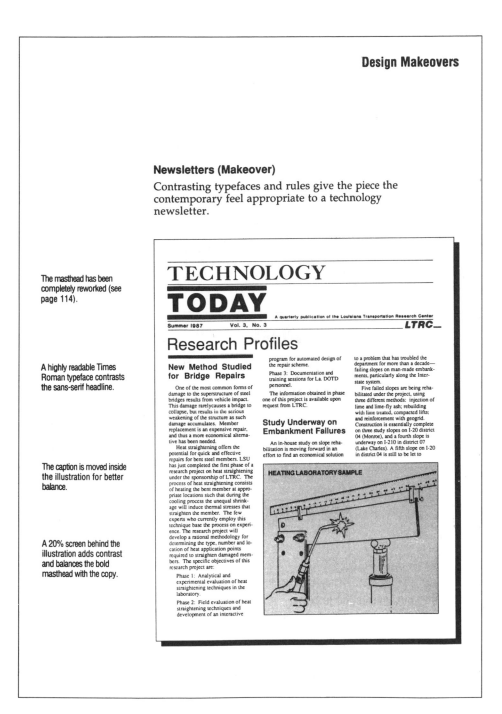

Design Makeovers

Newsletters (Makeover)
Contrasting typefaces and rules give the piece the contemporary feel appropriate to a technology newsletter.

The masthead has been completely reworked (see page 114).

A highly readable Times Roman typeface contrasts the sans-serif headline.

The caption is moved inside the illustration for better balance.

A 20% screen behind the illustration adds contrast and balances the bold masthead with the copy.

TECHNOLOGY
TODAY

A quarterly publication of the Louisiana Transportation Research Center

Summer 1987   Vol. 3, No. 3   **LTRC**

Research Profiles

New Method Studied for Bridge Repairs

One of the most common forms of damage to the superstructure of steel bridges results from vehicle impact. This damage rarely causes a bridge to collapse, but results in the serious weakening of the structure as such damage accumulates. Member replacement is an expensive repair, and thus a more economical alternative has been needed.

Heat straightening offers the potential for quick and effective repairs for bent steel members. LSU has just completed the first phase of a research project on heat straightening under the sponsorship of LTRC. The process of heat straightening consists of heating the bent member at appropriate locations such that during the cooling process the unequal shrinkage will induce thermal stresses that straighten the member. The few experts who currently employ this technique base the process on experience. The research project will develop a rational methodology for determining the type, number and location of heat application points required to straighten damaged members. The specific objectives of this research project are:

Phase 1: Analytical and experimental evaluation of heat straightening techniques in the laboratory.

Phase 2: Field evaluation of heat straightening techniques and development of an interactive

program for automated design of the repair scheme.

Phase 3: Documentation and training sessions for La. DOTD personnel.

The information obtained in phase one of this project is available upon request from LTRC.

Study Underway on Embankment Failures

An in-house study on slope rehabilitation is moving forward in an effort to find an economical solution

to a problem that has troubled the department for more than a decade—failing slopes on man-made embankments, particularly along the Interstate system.

Five failed slopes are being rehabilitated under the project, using three different methods: injection of lime and lime-fly ash; rebuilding with lime treated, compacted lifts; and reinforcement with geogrid. Construction is essentially complete on three study slopes on I-20 district 04 (Monroe), and a fourth slope is underway on I-210 in district 07 (Lake Charles). A fifth slope on I-20 in district 04 is still to be let to

HEATING LABORATORY SAMPLE

White space

Some information and messages can be enhanced by the use of graphics and white space. The two versions of the manual that follow both use graphics and white space.

Version 1

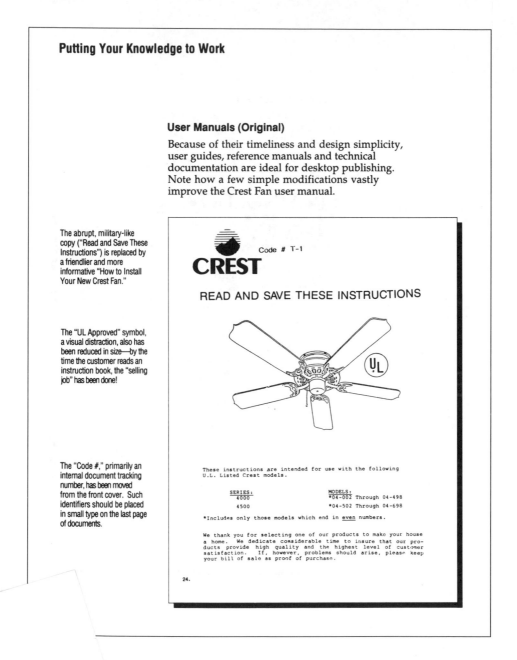

Putting Your Knowledge to Work

User Manuals (Original)

Because of their timeliness and design simplicity, user guides, reference manuals and technical documentation are ideal for desktop publishing. Note how a few simple modifications vastly improve the Crest Fan user manual.

The abrupt, military-like copy ("Read and Save These Instructions") is replaced by a friendlier and more informative "How to Install Your New Crest Fan."

The "UL Approved" symbol, a visual distraction, also has been reduced in size—by the time the customer reads an instruction book, the "selling job" has been done!

The "Code #," primarily an internal document tracking number, has been moved from the front cover. Such identifiers should be placed in small type on the last page of documents.

Code # T-1

CREST

READ AND SAVE THESE INSTRUCTIONS

These instructions are intended for use with the following U.L. Listed Crest models.

SERIES: MODELS:
  4000   *04-002 Through 04-498
  4500   *04-502 Through 04-698

*Includes only those models which end in *even* numbers.

We thank you for selecting one of our products to make your house a home. We dedicate considerable time to insure that our products provide high quality and the highest level of customer satisfaction. If, however, problems should arise, please keep your bill of sale as proof of purchase.

24.

Version 2 *Note the design features which make this version more eye-catching*

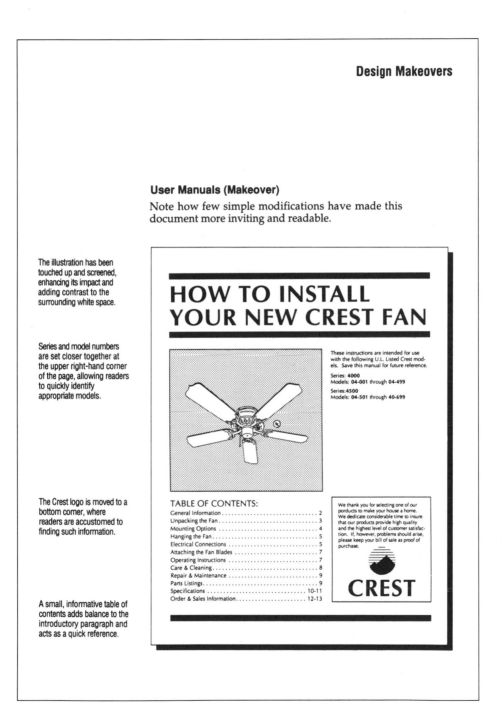

Design Makeovers

User Manuals (Makeover)

Note how few simple modifications have made this document more inviting and readable.

The illustration has been touched up and screened, enhancing its impact and adding contrast to the surrounding white space.

Series and model numbers are set closer together at the upper right-hand corner of the page, allowing readers to quickly identify appropriate models.

The Crest logo is moved to a bottom corner, where readers are accustomed to finding such information.

A small, informative table of contents adds balance to the introductory paragraph and acts as a quick reference.

HOW TO INSTALL YOUR NEW CREST FAN

These instructions are intended for use with the following U.L. Listed Crest models. Save this manual for future reference.

Series: **4000**
Models: **04-001** through **04-499**

Series: **4500**
Models: **04-501** through **40-699**

TABLE OF CONTENTS:

We thank you for selecting one of our porducts to make your house a home. We dedicate considerable time to insure that our products provide high quality and the highest level of customer satisfaction. If, however, problems should arise, please keep your bill of sale as proof of purchase.

CREST

Other forms of emphasis

> The following examples are taken from the *Network Educational Press* series of Study Guides.

Use of bold or italic fonts, screened text or symbols

How will the data be collected

⚠️ Make sure your teacher knows what you propose to do and
BE CAREFUL - ROADS ARE DANGEROUS.

Try to work in a group of four or more - it is **SAFER**, quicker and will allow you to gather lots of data in the time available.

If other groups do different traffic trouble spots then you could share your results - use the same methods at each location.

You are now ready to collect your data

© Network Educational Press

Boxes

A graphic line or box can also be very effective in emphasising certain information:

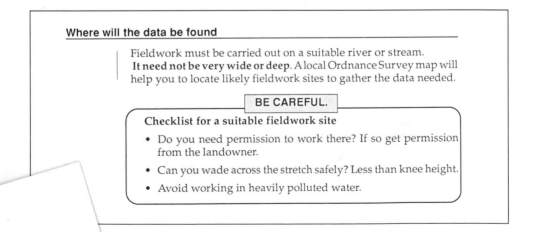

Where will the data be found

Fieldwork must be carried out on a suitable river or stream. **It need not be very wide or deep**. A local Ordnance Survey map will help you to locate likely fieldwork sites to gather the data needed.

BE CAREFUL.

Checklist for a suitable fieldwork site

- Do you need permission to work there? If so get permission from the landowner.
- Can you wade across the stretch safely? Less than knee height.
- Avoid working in heavily polluted water.

Graphics

Illustrations, graphs and tables can all help to make a document more interesting and attractive and less daunting. Some information is better in a diagram:

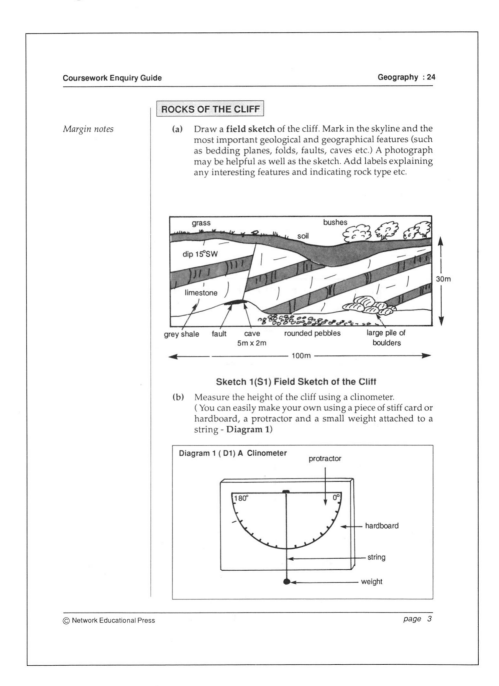

Visual models of how to record data can be very effective.

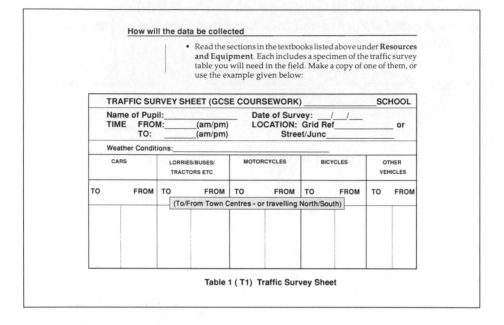

How will the data be collected

- Read the sections in the textbooks listed above under **Resources and Equipment**. Each includes a specimen of the traffic survey table you will need in the field. Make a copy of one of them, or use the example given below:

Table 1 (T1) Traffic Survey Sheet

An illustration of how to present results in graph form can give confidence to students required to provide similar information:

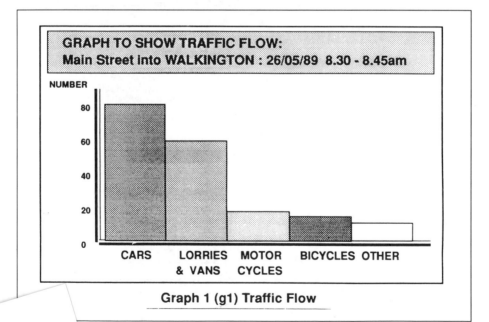

Graph 1 (g1) Traffic Flow

Cartoons

Many educational documents are now littered with cartoons. Used sparingly and in the right context they can lighten a document. If they are over-used, however, or placed in the wrong context they can patronise and irritate the reader.

This cartoon might lighten
a serious INSET day!

*The one below
would probably
offend!*

Others would disagree...

*Whatever your tastes in cartoons, a well designed document can enhance the message. Graphic designers would leave you with one message - **keep it simple!***

*This page (from Roger Parker's Looking Good in Print book) shows how a document littered with different forms of emphasis fails dismally to deliver its message; this disease is known as **fontitis!***

B

Desktop Publishing

All designs featured in this book can be achieved fairly simply using desktop publishing. Many schools and colleges will now have such facilities and will be using them to good effect. Others will have the necessary equipment and associated software but may not have provided the necessary training. Some may not be aware of the potential of the facility. This section of the chapter provides a *brief introduction* to those teachers *new* to the concept.

What is desktop publishing?

It is a form of typesetting which is carried out by a computer and which allows you to create a document of near professional quality.

What equipment is required?

All computer systems have desktop publishing capability. Some schools and colleges will have invested in IBM, some in Nimbus, others in Archimides and others in Apple. All can run desktop publishing programs.

The hardware is just one part of the system. The software is very important, and the market leaders in desktop publishing programs are Aldus *Pagemaker* and Rank Xerox *Ventura*. *Each has its particular strengths: Ventura* is renowned as a program for creating books or long documents, while *Pagemaker* is often described as a designer's program.

The best program for schools and colleges who want to produce a wide range of documents of different styles is, in our opinion, *Pagemaker.* The latest version, *Pagemaker 4*, used on an Apple Mac is quite stunning in its versatility, and now that the Apple education discounts have been introduced, the machines are worth looking at.

Can desktop publishing software be added to existing computer systems?

Yes it can, but caution is urged. Some local authorities have installed *Pagemaker* on the computer systems purchased to manage accounts under LMS. This is not a very good idea. Desktop publishing is ideally provided in a stand-alone machine. Teachers, technicians, ancillary staff and students who want access to the facility do not want to compete with others needing the system for other purposes - accounts, for example. A system devoted to desktop publishing would be in constant use and control over its use is more easily managed.

Are other equipment and software necessary?

Ideally, yes. Some of the more advanced desktop publishing systems have an integrated *word processing package*, but in most you will need a word processing program compatible with the desktop publishing software.

If you are planning to create professional looking documents it is advisable that you invest in a *laser printer*, which, ideally, should be situated with the desktop publishing system. It *is* possible to house the printer elsewhere and to take floppy disks to it for output, but in practice this is complicated and will discourage use of the system.

Most laser printers have only a limited range of fonts and type styles, and some features such as white text on a black background will not print out on them. If you can invest in a printer with *Postscript* facility you will have a wide range of fonts and styles.

What about graphics?

There are a number of software programs which allow you to create or import graphics. Another piece of equipment which will considerably enhance the desktop publishing facility is a *scanner.* A scanner is a machine rather like a photocopier which copies a graphic into the memory of a graphics program in the computer. This allows you to import a graphic of your choice into a document and then size it, crop it, change its shape, or edit it in whatever way you wish.   The relatively inexpensive *hand-held* scanners do not have all these functions, but the more expensive *flatbed* scanners are now very sophisticated.

Furthermore, a scanner will also allow you to *scan text* into the word processing package. The text-scanning software copies the text in, the spellchecker is used, and the text can then be imported into the desktop publishing program ready to set out. The advantage of this is that where someone with slow keyboard skills wants to prepare a document, it can be typed anywhere and the printout can be taken to the desktop publishing system without monopolising the machine for hours while *two fingers* type in the text.

How long does it take to learn to use?

There is no doubt that someone can learn to use a program from a manual, but it is not the best approach, especially if it is someone who is new to computers. Two days' training is usually recommended for both Ventura and Pagemaker, but the training needs to be followed up with regular *hands-on* experience. In this way it is possible for someone to be producing simple documents soon after training starts. The more advanced applications will come with practice (*and confidence!*).

What uses will a desktop publishing system have?

There are many. All schools and colleges are now looking to *market* themselves. Professional *brochures, newsletters* and *reports* can only enhance the image of the institution. This book has argued for the preparation of *quality assignments* and *study guides* rather than *in-house resources*. Good content is only half the battle - the documents must look attractive and desktop publishing provides the means to achieve it. *Differentiation* is also a major concern in this book, and the adaptation of activities and assignments for weak readers or those with poor eyesight, for example, is relatively simple on such a system.

How much will a desktop publishing system cost?

Costs will vary enormously depending on the equipment already available and the level of sophistication required. It is possible to purchase a basic system of computer with desktop publishing, word processing software and a laser printer for less than £2500. More sophisticated systems will cost in excess of £5000. It is advisable to ask for the equipment to be installed and configured by the company selling it - buying a box off the shelf can often cause problems if this process is not carried out properly.

Scanners vary from between £200 - £300 for the hand held variety to £600 - £800 for the flatbed. As with most equipment, the more you pay the more features are available and enormous *discounts* can be obtained by shopping around.

All major computer manufacturers are keen to corner the education market, so ask for special deals and try to get training included - it will be well worth it. If you are able to afford a *maintenance contract*, which usually costs about 8% - 10% extra, your equipment will be repaired or replaced with a loan machine within 24 hours. Guarantees alone are often no use if repairs take 3 months and you are without your equipment at crucial times.

Whatever system you choose, whatever price you pay, desktop publishing is a facility that all schools and colleges ought to have. It makes sense in so many ways, and in terms of simple economics. If 2 more students are attracted to your institution because of its professional image a £5000 system would pay for itself in less than three years.

Managing Resources

Practical Problems

The Library/Resource Centre

The Librarian Resource Centre Manager

MANAGING RESOURCES

Once teachers begin to use a wide variety of resources problems of *management* invariably arise.

This chapter examines:

A) the practical problems faced by teachers,

B) the role of the library/resource centre in supporting resource-based approaches

C) the role of the librarian/resource centre manager.

Practical problems

These problems come under a number of headings:

- numbers of resources
- access to resources
- storage of resources
- space in the classroom
- the problems faced by the 'peripatetic' teacher.

Numbers of resources

Once the resource collection is together the first task is to ensure that there are sufficient quantities of each resource to meet demand.

For example, in the assignments on Road Safety illustrated earlier, the text *Road Accidents in Britain* is obviously a *core* resource. There should ideally be enough copies for each student or at worst one between two. Other resources in the Road Safety collection may not be used by all students and smaller numbers of these - 5s or 6s for a class of 30, for example - may suffice.

There may be single copies of some items and here the teacher will have to ensure that it is used for an *enrichment* or *reinforcement* activity undertaken at intervals by only one or two students at a time.

Some schools organise their curriculum in such a way that a year group or half year follow the same course at the same time. If this happens the organisation of the Road Safety course, for example, is a massive undertaking. Large numbers of resources need to be made available and it is likely to be uneconomic.

In these circumstances it is likely that either (a) the resource collection is seriously impoverished in any one class room or (b) the department produces an in-house 'booklet' covering the key points and information - a cost saving measure.

Either way the quality of the provision is diminished. The alternative that many schools would adopt is to *modularise* the whole course and offer the Road Safety module at intervals throughout the year (or 2 years). Each class will cover the module, but at different times, and the richness of the resource provision is maintained.

There are sacrifices that have to be made, however. The 'lead lesson' with 4 classes, visitors and/or hire films cannot take place - both films and visitors will need to appear several times over. However, if such visitors can be persuaded to come more than once, the quality of the interaction will almost certainly improve if only 30 as opposed to 100 students are involved.

The argument for the modular approach is a strong one. It is cost effective; colleagues within a department can pass on both resources and advice; and the collection of resources can be rich and varied.

Access to resources

Once the collection is complete and before the assignments are prepared, most resources will need to be *labelled*: (Resource item *A, B, C* or *1, 2, 3* etc.) A small sticky label on the spine or cover of a book, for example, will suffice.

Storage facilities need to be provided - for many resource items the magazine box (see the illustration below) is ideal.

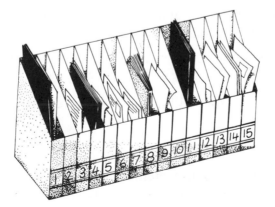

Storage boxes can be purchased quite cheaply in strong cardboard, but for long term use the indestructible plastic version is more costly but preferable. Plastic trays can fulfil a similar purpose.

Peripherals, such as pens, paper, rulers etc., should be stored in boxes or trays as appropriate. A simple checking system will need to be set up. Teachers of Technology have always used such checking systems for equipment and tools.

In a classroom this collection might then be placed on a table, or better still, a trolley (see illustration below).

The trolley fulfils a number of functions:

- it can store a larger quantity of resource items
- it can be moved quickly and easily to other classrooms (if on the same level) or to storage areas
- it can be moved quickly if space is needed for activities such as role play.

The question of access from a library or resource centre is dealt with in part B below.

Storage of resources

In Book 2 of this series, Philip Waterhouse stresses the importance of *storage* in the classroom. He argues that only those resources in current use should be stored in the classroom itself.

Many teachers, however, find themselves unable to meet this desirable aim . Tables, desks, cupboards, filing cabinets are full of resources, some in use, some about to be used and some that never will be used.

A number of avenues can be explored:

- the modular approach will mean that 'sets' of resources only reside in a classroom when in use

- a thorough 'clear out' will free space for essential items

- the purchase of library boxes will provide tidy and easily accessed storage on shelves

- the fitting of shelving high on classroom walls will provide storage that does not reduce students' working spaces

- the conversion of redundant toilet or cloakroom areas can provide valuable long-term storage areas.

Some teachers will find other ways to provide storage but time spent on this is an *investment*. The confusion and muddle that can arise when a large number of resources are being used but not properly stored will quickly *push teachers back to the simplicity and safety of the single text*.

Space in the classroom

The classroom where a variety of activities are contemplated and a range of resources are in use will need to be flexible.

The room arrangement must facilitate:

- whole class work

- group work

- independent work

- practical activity.

Students who are using resources must be able to *move freely* to collect or return resources, and the arrangement of tables and desks must allow a simple and speedy change from independent to group work.

Philip Waterhouse deals in detail with this issue in Book 2 of the series, *Classroom Management*, but one of his suggestions for using space is included here. *(See diagram overleaf.)*

If rooms do not allow free movement, if tables or desks are constantly being moved, then the classroom atmosphere will be seriously impaired.

The 'Workstation' Layout

The Peripatetic Teacher

Many teachers will have the luxury of their own classroom - a base over which they have a large degree of control. It is the ideal situation. The arrangement of the furniture, the decoration and display in the room, the storage systems are all variables in classroom and resource management.

A significant number of teachers - particularly in FE - have no such luxury. They teach in a variety of *all purpose* classrooms, have no influence or control over layout, decor or storage, and worse still are able to use *only those resources which they are able to carry with them.*

The idea that specialist classrooms are only needed by science, design and technology is outdated. If teachers are to be able to use resources in the ways described earlier the use of a 'base' is essential. The 'base' can be shared between a number of teachers but it is essential that they co-operate over furniture arrangement, resource storage and display.

Greater stress needs to be placed on this point by both senior managers in the timetabling and by middle managers who can often influence such decisions.

For example the Department of seven with four specialist bases can often mean full-time teachers have their own room and part-timers, the Deputy Head teaching a little English for example, are peripatetic. The Head of Department can insist, in this situation, that all seven share the specialist bases - with each teacher in a non-specialist room for a small proportion of their timetable. The *peripatetics* can then take advantage of the specialist accommodation like others in the Department. There are a variety of solutions to this problem, but one thing is clear: if teachers remain peripatetic they will be forced to adopt *narrow* approaches and make *limited* use of resources.

B ## The library/resource centre

There is no doubt that LMS and a desire on the part of Government to reduce the proportion of the funds held centrally by Local Authorities is going to put the existence and function of the library service at risk. That this should be so is ludicrous. The introduction of GCSE, the National Curriculum, TVEI, the proposals for NVQ and the post-16 core skills, all demand a well resourced and active library/resource service. This section of the chapter examines the contribution that can and should be made by such services.

The role of the library/resource centre.

The well resourced and fully staffed resource centre plays a central, co-ordinating role within schools and colleges. It provides:

- a wide variety of resources, including books, periodicals, AVA, IT facility, database information
- an area for quiet private study, group enquiry and discussion, practical activity
- a central resource to be used by all members of the community: students, teachers, parents, governors, and other community groups.

It helps to develop:

- information and data handling skills
- research skills
- a passion for books.

Accommodation and equipment

A library or resource centre which plays such a role will ideally require flexible accommodation and extensive equipment:

- enough accommodation to seat comfortably a minimum of 10% of the student population at any one time
- areas set aside for quiet, private study

- areas where groups can meet, talk and plan

- areas where library/resource centre users can undertake practical activity such as planning, designing and pasting up booklets

- areas where users can privately watch videos, listen to audio tapes or undertake video or audio recordings

- areas where users can interrogate a database, use a software program and have access to desktop publishing.

This is, of course, the ideal, but not, as some would suggest, unrealistic. Many schools and colleges provide such accommodation. Many local authorities have placed great emphasis on the development of such library/resource centres.

In West Glamorgan, for instance, all secondary schools have been funded, through TVEI, to develop resource centre provision.

Michael Hunt, Deputy Head of St. Joseph's School, Port Talbot, was seconded in 1987, and part of his brief was to plan the 'ideal' accommodation. The diagram below illustrates the plans that emerged - working, as the school was, within the confines of the existing buildings and the finance allocated.

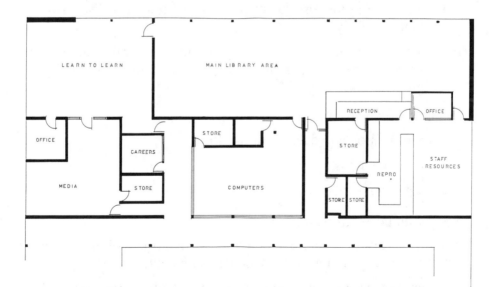

C The role of the librarian/resource centre manager

The term 'library' is used to describe widely differing provision.   HMI in 1988 reported.

> Libraries were in general the weakest aspect of the schools' resources....the provision and use of libraries are matters for considerable concern....secondary school libraries should be stocked on the basis of 10 books per pupil....Among the schools inspected some had 3 or fewer whilst a fortunate few libraries had collections which contained 20 or more books per pupil.

(Secondary Schools: An Appraisal by HMI. HMSO 1988)

The position of *librarians* also differs widely - from the school with one or more full time Chartered Librarian - some with additional ancillary support - to the school which allocates the Teacher Librarian one free period a week for library work.

The advice which follows, therefore, on the role of the librarian or resource manager, in no way underestimates the scale of the task. Some schools which have allowed the library provision to deteriorate over many years face the prospect of major investment if they are to come anywhere near the examples of good practice that exist. The Teacher Librarian reading this who has lost one or two periods a week can be forgiven if this section appears in the realms of *cloud cuckoo land*.

The Librarian can play a number of key roles.

Resource management

All major curriculum initiatives of the past few years have emphasised the need for a wide ranging use of resources. A resource manager is in a unique position of being able to oversee developments across faculties or departments and to minimise duplication and repetition.

Information management

Information skills is a central theme of curriculum development and the librarian will have a key role in setting up systems which allow students and staff easy and efficient access to a wide range of information, including on-line databases such as MARIS or NERIS. There is also a strong case for the librarian to play a role in the management of the mountain of information that regularly arrives on the desks of senior management.

Librarians have skills in the storage, collection, retrieval and dissemination of information and once LMS is fully implemented this kind of *information management* would be enormously helpful.

Curriculum Development

Librarians all over the country will be familiar with the following scene:

> Monday morning period 2. Two 13 year olds arrive in the library with a library slip.
>
> "We've got to do a project on pollution. Have you got any books which might help us?"

The scene varies - sometimes it's 30 or more asking for the same books, sometimes it's a whole year group during the same few weeks.

Few librarians, it would appear, are involved in curriculum planning, and the first indication they have of particular investigation topics or themes is when hordes of students walk through the doors.

If librarians had the status of Heads of Department, and were invited to attend departmental curriculum planning sessions, this scenario would disappear. Librarians would then be able to assist in a number of ways. They could:

- plan for particular topics and themes, bringing in resources from a wide range of sources

- counsel students working in the library as an informed but non-specialist *tutor*

- advise departments of other resources/information that might be useful

- identify any potential duplication ("we did that in History yesterday")

- support departments in the creation of study guides (see Chapter 5).

There are many schools where the librarian fulfils this kind of role and it fits particularly well in institutions where teamwork is emphasised.

Counselling/tutoring

Many librarians play a major role in supporting students working independently or in groups within the library. Large numbers of students need to undertake research for both projects and coursework and many find the task daunting. Teachers everywhere will identify with the problems of the *project* which contains large chunks of text copied faithfully, but uncritically, from the first reference book the student finds. When projects are clearly defined and contain specified objectives, non-specialist adults such as librarians are able to support students working independently. Where *study guides* are in use librarians are able to understand *what* the student is doing, *where* the research is going and what kinds of *resources* are going to be helpful. The support they can offer students is invaluable.

If a librarian is to fulfil these wide ranging roles then it is clear that some care needs to be taken in deciding what kind of appointment to make.

The Teacher Librarian

There are many highly professional and dedicated teacher librarians whose time allowance varies from one or two periods a week to the half timetable. Such people may have the *skills* to fulfil many of the roles described but it is doubtful whether they will have the *time*. Their commitment to their teaching must remain a priority, and involvement in curriculum planning with other departments will be problematic. Few teacher librarians will have specific training in information skills and many will regard their role as book managers. They will perform this task assiduously, many with only small time allowances.

Working as a link person between management, departments and students is a demanding role. It will require someone with a dynamic and outgoing personality. Not all Teacher Librarians will fit this description and some will simply shudder at the prospect. Another problem of the Teacher Librarian is that in some instances libraries are unsupervised or locked at times when they are unavailable. There are examples of superbly stocked and resourced libraries which, sadly, are only open at lunchtimes or after school.

The untrained adult/parent

Many successful school libraries are run by untrained but committed adults - some parents - and there are numerous instances of school libraries being transformed through the sheer enthusiasm and energy of such people (some even working on a voluntary basis).

There is no doubt that for many of the roles outlined earlier the enthusiast with the right personality could be an ideal choice - particularly if training can be offered by the Schools Library Service.

There are weaknesses in this approach, of course. Some untrained librarians would be reluctant to attend departmental meetings, and in some cases teaching staff might have reservations about how much an untrained teacher or librarian might contribute. Using voluntary labour is also tricky. The demands on librarians are enormous and are likely to increase. It is doubtful whether someone working voluntarily can be asked to take on such additional burdens.

The 'team' approach

Some schools appoint a Teacher Librarian with overall responsibility for the library, and then timetable a team of staff who 'share' the duties of monitoring and supervision. This allows the library or resource centre to be open at all times and this is to be applauded.

Unfortunately, few timetablers are able to choose the ideal 'team' and some staff inevitably will see such a role as a burden. Their involvement will be superficial - *keeping an eye open* while marking - and the role of counsellor/tutor will be rejected. Nevertheless, if a small team of committed staff can be assembled, the chances of keeping the library fully open and staffed is increased. This is infinitely preferable to the closed doors policy. Counselling/tutoring will be possible in this arrangement, but it is unlikely if the 'team' can fulfil other roles.

The Chartered Librarian

The number of Chartered Librarians working in schools and colleges is increasing, with some LEAs boasting a Chartered Librarian in every secondary school.

There is no doubt that investment in such an appointment can pay off. In those schools where Chartered Librarians have worked for several years there would be uproar if the post were to disappear under LMS: the staff have come to realise the value of a full-time qualified librarian and full use is made of both the librarian and the facilities.

There is a *Catch 22* here, however. Many managers would hesitate before committing funds to such an appointment because in their schools the library is a *white elephant* - underused and understocked.

> The most serious weaknesses were that libraries were divorced from other resources, they were on the periphery of curricular planning and subject departments made little use of them in their routine work.

(Secondary Schools: An Appraisal by HMI. HMSO 1988)

Until departments see the intrinsic value of the library and start integrating its use within their own curricula, a Chartered Librarian would be a luxury.

Yet the presence of a skilled professional, able to provide INSET in the use of the library, would almost certainly hasten the process of change. The decision to appoint a full-time Chartered Librarian has already been made by hundreds of schools.

If more schools are to follow suit the main task for managers is to establish a whole school policy towards information skills. Once that is put in place and supported by INSET of various kinds, the need for such a post will become evident.

The decision that is then made to fund such an appointment will be a rational one supported by the majority of departments able to accept a small cut in their own allowances.

One final problem then arises. The pay and conditions of service of library staff are not good. Recruitment is a problem and if such people are to have the status of a Head of Department then they should have better pay and conditions.

Resource centres v classroom resource bases

The final section of this chapter examines a debate which is frequently heard once resource *empires* are created. *Should all resources be held centrally or should they be devolved?*

Yes and no, Minister, is the answer.

There is a great deal of sense in having some resources held centrally, and some devolved. Many resources that are expensive to purchase and which are used by different departments ought to be held centrally, as should the wide range of fiction and non-fiction books commonly found in libraries.

There is also a case for having a range of audio-visual and computer equipment held centrally - large 'capital' items like videos are a huge drain on individual departmental budgets.

But good classroom management is about *simple and easy access to resources,* and schools and colleges should resist the temptation to house all resources in some grand resource centre.

Using information v finding information

It has been argued that if resources are held centrally students will quickly acquire information as they search for the resources they need.

There is some truth in this, but there are also dangers. If the objectives of a particular assignment are to develop the skills of *searching* for appropriate resources then the approach of sending students to the resource centre is sound. If the assignment is completely *open-ended* and the teacher wants them to make use of as wide a variety of sources as possible, then a visit to the resource centre is sensible.

On the other hand if the objectives of an assignment are to develop the skills of *synthesis*, *analysis*, or *interpretation* of data, then the act of sending students to collect the resources is an unnecessary and time-consuming activity. In this case the student needs the resources at hand and there is a strong case, therefore, for the classroom resource base.

Librarians who are involved in curriculum planning will be more than willing to search for, collect and loan a set of relevant resources to a classroom resource base. Once the topic is finished, the on-loan resources return to their central base.

The centre v devolved debate need not become an issue. It is a straightforward matter to determine what is held where and no hard or fast 'rules' should be established which are to the detriment of individual department needs. Some departments, for example, make heavy use of video, or of IT equipment, and it would be sensible if they had their own. Common sense can usually prevail in those matters.

The way ahead

Let HMI have the final word here.

> There are disturbing disparities in provision which do not sit well alongside the best intentions of the National Curriculum. Although advances have been made, there are still many pupils who are paying the price of past neglect. It is still true to say, as in the 1985 HMI Report, that the investment of money, staff and time in some libraries is so low that without changes of policy, perception and levels of provision it will be difficult for those pupils to receive their full library and information skills entitlement.

(A Survey of Secondary School Libraries in Six Local Education Authorities. DES 1990)

Getting Started

Planning
Time
INSET

GETTING STARTED

There are those in the media who would argue that any move towards greater flexibility in the classroom is a move towards a 'free and easy', *laissez-faire* approach.

Nothing is further from the truth.

If you have read this far you will be aware that the ideas expressed in this book can only be delivered with careful planning, a great deal of time and INSET support.

These three issues, **Planning, Time** and **INSET** are the focus of the final chapter.

A   ## Planning

Institutional policy

There are many examples from all over the country of teachers, working in isolation, who have successfully implemented the kinds of approaches advocated in this book. It will not have been easy for them. Some will have encountered *resistance*, some *passive support* while others will have received real *encouragement*. But for all, the process will have involved long hours, dogged determination and moments of both elation and despair. Pioneers in any field will empathise with this. The isolated development, however, tends to be *owned* by the individuals, and developments disappear when they move to new posts.

The organisational constraints of timetables, rooms and resources hit these pioneers hardest because innovation generally requires institutional change. Some teachers, as Eric Hoyle points out, 'have to knock off the corners of an innovation to get it through the doors of the school'.

There is no doubt, therefore, that the long term development of student responsibility and autonomy requires an institutional approach. This does not mean, however, that all teachers, departments or faculties will move at the same time or at the same pace. Indeed, there is a strong case for small scale development, building on confidence, experience and strengths.

What is important, however, is that the general ethos and stated aims of the organisation provide a firm foundation for the developments in individual classrooms or departments.

An institution needs to set out clearly and unequivocally its philosophy with regard to:

- personal achievement

- teaching and learning styles

- information skills.

- the role of the library/resource centre

- differentiation

- recording and assessment

- inter-personal relationships

- cross-curricular themes and issues

- community links.

If these areas are the subject of clear policy statements drawn up after consultation with governors, parents, teachers and students then the detailed planning of departments and facilities is given greater direction.

The policy statement that is drawn up will almost certainly include guidelines on cross-curricular themes. How these guidelines are implemented will require further policy decisions.

There are two broad choices.

1) Cross-curricular themes are delivered through discrete modules as part of either (a) a tutorial programme (b) Social and Personal Education or (c) through courses such as General Studies. Some institutions may have a combination of these, depending upon, for example, the age group of the students.

2) Cross-curricular themes are integrated or *embedded* within the curriculum and delivered by departments through the medium of the subject or vocational course.

These are not mutually exclusive choices, of course. Institutions may choose to deliver some cross-curricular themes as discrete modules, and others through the existing curriculum.

Whichever approach is chosen, departments will need to be absolutely clear on what is expected so that their curriculum planning can build in what is required. The suggestions on departmental curriculum planning which follow assume that the second model has been chosen. There is a trend towards integration and away from the 'bolt-on' approach.

Racism being *taught* on weeks 2-4 in the year 10 Personal and Social Education course is plainly ludicrous. Many such courses are seen both by students and teachers as meaningless in a system where *valuable* courses are those that lead to accreditation.

It is very difficult, also, to bring about real understanding, empathy or attitude change in 'one-off' modules of this kind. The *Skills for Adolescence* course recognises, for example, that drugs education is about the long term development of personal self esteem. The same philosophy applies to issues as *Racism, Sexism, Health Education, Economic* and *Environmental Awareness, Careers Guidance* and *Information Technology*. They should all be part of a 'spiral' curriculum, regularly appearing in a variety of contexts throughout the educational process.

Post-16 there is a similar debate on *entitlement* and *core skills*. The National Curriculum Council proposes that the five National Curriculum cross-curricular themes should continue post-16:

- economic and industrial understanding
- environmental education
- education for citizenship
- careers education and guidance
- health education.

It is proposed that there should be two additional themes:

- scientific and technical understanding
- aesthetic and creative understanding.

The National Curriculum Council has also identified six core skills for the post-16 curriculum:

- communication
- problem solving
- personal skills
- numeracy
- information technology
- modern foreign languages.

How much of this can or should be integrated within the existing curriculum is a question being explored in thousands of institutions all over the country. It is clear that many of the themes and skills *can* be delivered through existing courses, but it will take detailed planning by both management and departments if the proposals are to be realised.

Departmental curriculum planning

Once institutional policy is set and decisions have been made on the delivery of cross-curricular themes and core skills, departments will be well placed to plan their curriculum.

The planning framework that follows provides a structure which will allow individual teachers, teams or departments to explore the ideas expressed earlier in the book. The framework assumes that teachers will want to tread cautiously, starting with one or two 'modules' or topics with one or two classes. The framework will, nevertheless, allow for large scale developments.

Planning a module - a possible strategy.

1) Decide upon the class or classes

2) Select a module or topic

3) Set objectives in terms of:

- knowledge

- understanding

- skills

- attitudes

- experiences

4) Identify resources

5) Decide on the main features of module

6) Devise a range of varied and differentiated assignments

7) Decide on how the module will be recorded and assessed

8) Consider problems of organisation

9) Trial the module

10) Evaluate the module

Each of the 10 stages is now explored in more detail.

1) Decide upon the class or classes.

Choose a group that is well motivated. Build up confidence and expertise with this kind of group before using new approaches with more difficult groups.

If teachers want INSET funding for the development from TVE they will need to work within the 14-18 age group.

You may prefer, however, to start with younger students and build on the skills they bring with them from junior schools.

2) Select a module or topic.

Some topics or themes lend themselves to a variety of approaches. Choose one that does and one that fits within the existing syllabus - do not waste time planning a module that is not, for example, part of the National Curriculum.

3) Set objectives

Knowledge and understanding

The National Curriculum, the syllabus, the assessment criteria will help teachers to plot these objectives.

Skills

Some skills will be defined in the National Curriculum and in the syllabus. Teachers should also identify cross-curricular skills such as *communication, numeracy, information technology* and *problem solving*. The institutional guidelines should also be consulted in drawing up a list of skills.

Attitudes

The National Curriculum, the syllabus and the institutional guidelines will be sources of guidance here - phrases such as *tolerance, perseverance,* and *positive approaches* will appear regularly in such documents.

A study of the cross-curricular themes will also suggest objectives related to *Equal Opportunities, Health Education, Environmental Education* and so on.

Experiences

Here teachers can consider objectives related to experiences such as *working with adults other than teachers, links with the community or industry, using information technology* or *working co-operatively as part of a group.*

4) Identify resources

In chapter 3 a wide range of resources were defined.

Teachers should begin their search for resources to support this module *in* the institution. If assignments are prepared independently of resources, as suggested, then existing texts, information booklets, videos, software, reference materials, etc. can all be accessed.

The Librarian/Resource Officer should be consulted and may search for other resources using County Library Service or databases. People and organisations which might contribute to the module should also be noted.

At this particular stage of the planning process **all** potential resources should be identified - *quality control* comes later.

5) Decide on the main features of module

With the best will in the world it will not be possible to deliver all objectives within one module.

Whole class work, group work, individual work; oral presentation, problem solving, active learning; using IT, equipment, video, library, museum; working with adults, businesses, community groups; addressing equal opportunities, health education, environmental issues ... the list is endless.

Students can develop this wide range of skills over a long period, but not necessarily in one module.

Teachers should decide at this stage *which* features are relevant to *this* module. Other features can be delivered in later modules.

6) Devise a range of varied and differentiated assignments

How will the module be introduced? How will students be fired with enthusiasm? Then think about follow-up activities:

- devise activities and assignments which will be core

- create assignments which will challenge and stretch those who cope well with core activities

- provide assignments which can provide reinforcement and success for those who experience difficulty

- vary activities and assignments to provide different styles of learning

- provide opportunities for whole class, small group and independent work.

Set out a brief plan like the one on page 43. Does it seem to provide variety and balance?

7) *Decide on how the module will be recorded and assessed*

What kinds of assessment will be used?

- written or oral tests?

- self-assessment?

- peer assessment?

- negotiated assessment?

- external assessment?

What kinds of records will be kept? Who will keep them?

- individual profile kept by teacher?

- profile kept by student?

- mark book?

- computer records?

- a combination of methods?

These decisions need to be made at the planning stage. Methods of assessment can then be included when assignments are planned and written.

8) *Consider problems of organisation*

Organisational considerations come under a number of headings:

. classroom	. labelling	. work outside the classroom
. use of space	. access	. safety
. furniture arrangement	. retrieval	. planning
. communication with colleagues (shared rooms)	. storage	. communication with parents
	. communication with library	. timetable cover
. resources	. equipment	
	. technical support	

Such issues need to be addressed if the module is to run smoothly.

9) Trial the module

Once the planning is complete the module needs to be trialled. Teachers should endeavour to see it through even if there are problems initially. Some teachers and students may find aspects of the trial unsettling and unfamiliar and time should be allowed for both to adjust to the new demands.

10) Evaluate the module

At the end of the module every effort should be made to evaluate it:

Objectives

Were the stated objectives in terms of student learning achieved?

Activities

Were the activities appropriate, well received and sufficiently varied? Do other approaches need to be explored?

Differentiation

Were the assignments sufficiently differentiated? Were the most able challenged? Did any students fail to achieve? Do any assignments need to be adapted or adjusted in the light of experience?

Organisation

Were there any problems related to the organisation? Access to resources? Use of space? Communication with others? Technical problems?

B Time

It will be very surprising if teachers reading this have not at some time thought to themselves:

> *When can I find time for such detailed planning?*

Indeed, stronger language will probably have been used!

When politicians argue over what teachers need most to raise the morale of the profession the most frequent phrases used are *higher pay, greater status, smaller classes, better maintained buildings*. Few mention **time.**

The rate of change in the past 10 years has been frightening. Each new initiative demands a re-assessment of priorities, long meetings to formulate policy and, almost inevitably, longer hours in preparation and planning.

The proposals in this book are no different. There will be teachers saying at this point: *I would have been doing all of this if I had more time*.

Successful implementation of more flexible styles of teaching and learning requires detailed planning. Time is once again at a premium. Readers might reflect for a few moments and ask themselves how often they have been required to introduce new initiatives without additional time. Some courses on *stress management* try to persuade teachers to respond to senior management with replies such as:

> *Yes, I am prepared to take on this initiative, but what would you like me to give up first?*

This is one kind of solution but not one that will be readily acceptable to many teachers or one that is respected by all managers.

There are other ways to create time.

Meeting time

In many institutions a good deal of time is wasted. Readers will no doubt be able to think of many examples of meetings which were badly managed - the classic example of this is illustrated in the John Cleese training video *Meetings, Bloody Meetings*.

There is a strong case for keeping meetings to a minimum. Managers must try to protect staff from the pointless meetings where agendas are loose and where discussion goes round in circles. This leads to frustration and more importantly uses up time that might have been used more productively.

Buying time

The changes in education in recent years have given both schools and colleges greater flexibility in the management of resources. For some this has brought hardship for reasons that are well documented and there will be a period when managers will be overly cautious in committing funds to anything but the basic necessities.

Time is a necessity, however, and as institutions become more experienced in managing budgets confidence will grow and time can be created. Devolved budgets are, of course, already being used to create time.

Remitted time

Many institutions now allocate time to individuals who have some kind of curricular responsibility. This can be funded from the staffing, INSET or TVE budgets but the primary aim is to give individuals time to develop initiatives (eg. TVE), a course or a policy (eg. Equal Opportunities).

Secondment

Secondment is the traditional route through which teachers find time for *refreshment* and further training. The numbers of staff allowed the luxury of a year's secondment to work for a higher degree, for example, is falling. Once financial management is wholly delegated to the institution this type of secondment will become increasingly rare.

The short term secondment, pioneered by Tim Brighouse in Oxfordshire, and further developed by authorities such as Leeds, Leicestershire, Northamptonshire and Somerset will be far more common.   Here staff were seconded for one or two days a week to develop strategies, courses or policy specific to the needs of institutions or consortia.

Short courses

One of the most common ways to use budgets to create time is to release staff for the short course. Cover may be arranged internally but more often supply teachers are used.

Short courses provide opportunities for teachers to enhance existing skills, to learn new ones and to keep abreast of new developments.

Using budgets to provide individuals with *remitted time*, *secondment* or a place on a *short course* is a useful strategy and one that will continue to be widely used.

There are a number of weaknesses to these approaches, however.

Remitted time is normally allocated to individuals. While they may find the time invaluable the work they do may have little effect on the vast majority of colleagues who themselves have no extra time. There is a danger in this situation that the idea or project being developed is the 'responsibility' of that individual when in fact it has implications for all staff.

Secondment is also extremely valuable to the individuals concerned. The high relative cost of a one year or one term secondment, however, means that very few teachers will benefit and, as with remitted time, seconded teachers are sometimes seen as the 'experts' and no-one else feels inclined to take on responsibility for innovation.

The *short course* provides teachers with an opportunity to learn new skills and to advance their thinking but it does not create time. Indeed, staff absent on short courses are invariably asked to set the work for their classes and mark it on their return. They end up having less time.

Supply teachers do a professional job in difficult circumstances, but many are asked simply to be 'minders', and this situation cannot easily be justified.

Short courses do not always meet the needs of individuals or institutions.   Many, however, will be so good that teachers return to their institutions fired with enthusiasm and with a determination to implement the newly discovered ideas or skills. They soon find that the necessary planning time is not there. The ideas go into 'cold storage'.

The use of budgets for *remitted time, secondment* or *short courses*, therefore, is valuable but does not provide the planning time that is really needed. *Individuals*, it would seem, can benefit: *teams* of teachers cannot.

The team approach

There are ways that teams of teachers can be given small amounts of time. One 'model' of this operates as follows:

Stage 1   Senior Management identify key areas for development eg. teaching and learning styles, use of IT, integration of the library, records of achievement and equal opportunities.

Stage 2   The Senior Management offers a series of 0.1 'secondments'. (How many will depend on how much money can be allocated.)

Stage 3   Faculties, Departments or cross-curricular teams are invited to 'bid' for any of these 0.1 secondments. The bid must demonstrate how the curriculum will be developed so as to incorporate the criteria set out in Stage 1.

Stage 4   Particular 'bids' are submitted, negotiated then accepted.

Stage 5   The extra 0.1 on the timetable gives the successful departments an extra member of staff one morning or afternoon a week throughout the year.

Stage 6   Every Thursday morning in, for example, Science, there are six timetabled classes with seven teachers. (The seventh 'floating' teacher is a result of the extra 0.1.)

Stage 7   The Science Department meets as a team to plan a module, theme or topic, and plan together up to point 5 of the planning framework on page 107.

Stage 8   The detailed planning of differentiated activities and assignments, the assessment strategies and organisational problems are now developed by the 'floating' teacher. He/she can stay at home, for example, every Thursday morning for three or four weeks.

Stage 9   The module is now ready to trial. The floating teacher (teacher A) trials it on this Thursday morning with the class of teacher B. This short module lasts for three or four Thursday morning lessons. Teacher B observes all those lessons.

Stage 10   The Science Department meets again to plan a second module.

Stage 11   Teacher B is now off timetable on Thursday mornings. Teacher A takes over all his/her classes and being a specialist is responsible for setting the work and marking it.

Stage 12   Teacher B develops the assignments, activities, and assessment strategies and sorts out the organisational problems. After three or four weeks he/she trials it with teacher C. Teacher C observes.

Stage 13   Teacher A now takes over the Thursday morning classes of teacher C, teacher B returns to his/her groups. Teacher C develops a third module and trials it with teacher D observing.

And so on...

In this way it would be possible, with the right timetable structure, to allow up to **six** teachers to have one morning a week for half a term each.

At the end of a year the department would have 6 short modules designed to incorporate those characteristics identified by Management in Stage 1.

There are many advantages to this arrangement:

- a *team* of teachers shares the single 0.1. The morale of the team is raised

- planning and evaluation becomes a team activity

- paired teaching allows observation of classroom management, tutoring skills etc. Confidence can be raised and resistance overcome if teachers can actually observe others working. Pairings can reflect levels of experience, confidence etc.

- the modules that are produced are INSET modules and it is likely that future planning and curriculum development will mirror the good practice they have engendered

- INSET funds are targeted - *woolly* bids will be unsuccessful. Clearer thinking and planning will be encouraged

- a rolling programme over a number of years might give every department or faculty a similar secondment

- teachers' general morale will be raised because management is not only saying "this development is important" but also providing time for it to be implemented.

The 'model' described here has been used successfully by a number of schools and its main principles can be adapted to a variety of situations.

It has its weaknesses, of course. No strategy is perfect:

- some institutions will have small departments where a 'floating' teacher will be impractical

- some specialisms are already understaffed - finding 'extra' will be impossible

- some timetable structures will not permit such an arrangement

- some institutions will not be able to afford it.

The question of cost really concerns policy. If the curriculum planning framework on pages 107 - 111 is used, the need for responsibility allowances and remitted time for areas such as equal opportunities, records of achievement, health education, is called into question.

If it becomes institution policy that such themes are integrated within all curriculum areas then these posts are unnecessary. Specialist 'consultant' support can be hired to support teams and all funds saved can be channelled to support curriculum development.

The need for managers to create time is a priority. Whether they do it in the way described or in other imaginative ways, it should be found.

Without it, real, long term change will be a slow process, and *courses for teacher stress will become a growth industry.*

 INSET

Creating the time for detailed planning will be of little use if staff have neither the understanding, inclination nor the skills to profit from it. A major task for management is therefore the creation of an effective programme of In-Service Training.

Some aspects of INSET have already been dealt with under the headings of *planning* and *time*. There are several other strategies, however, which might usefully be mentioned here.

Raising awareness

The need for change is often not recognised by all staff. An analysis of National Curriculum guidelines, TVE criteria, assessment procedures, HMI reports and so on, will provide a mountain of evidence. Many staff, however, will never read such documents and it is the task of managers and middle managers to summarise key points. They can then be used persuasively in curriculum planning. The presentation of such ideas in staff meetings will be less successful.

If department or faculty teams use curriculum planning time to solve the problems of implementing initiatives such as the National Curriculum, for example, awareness comes *naturally* and *in context.*

Setting a policy for teaching and learning

In Book 2, *Classroom Management*, Philip Waterhouse argues persuasively that curriculum teams ought to set their own 'policy for teaching'.

He sets out a whole of set of criteria by which teachers might evaluate their own practice in the classroom.

He suggests that the criteria ought to be seen as a starting point for teams to set up their own, and that this process would lead to a policy for teaching and learning.

The activities he puts forward are pure INSET. The policy that teams draw up will be their own and will reflect not only the needs of the curriculum and the institution, but the needs of individuals who will be encouraged to move as far as they feel able at a particular time.

Mutual observation

In the same book, *Classroom Management*, Philip Waterhouse also highlights the value of mutual observation. In the early years of the Avon Resources for Learning Project there were some teachers who were doubtful if the approaches being suggested and the resources being developed would work for them.

That wouldn't work with my kids was the comment of one teacher at the time and Philip Waterhouse and his team countered this by offering to teach in classrooms where teachers wanted to observe the resources and approaches in use.

Nearly 30 *demonstrations* were arranged in Avon at that time - some lasting for up to six or eight lessons. Members of departments observed in a rota and were later encouraged to experiment themselves.

There is no doubt that the *demonstrations* provided teachers with a better understanding than any meeting or INSET course could have done.

'Demonstration' lessons are not being advocated here. But opportunities for staff to work closely with colleagues and to observe and be observed teaching should be provided - see Book 2 in this series for suggestions on how this might work.

Teacher Development Days

The five 'Baker' days in schools are invariably booked up well in advance, such are the demands on time.

Many Managers organise these days on a thematic basis - *Teaching and Learning Styles, Records of Achievement, Industrial Awareness, National Curriculum* and so on.

In some institutions the teacher development days provide an opportunity for the staff to come together to share ideas and expertise (see Book 5, Tim Brighouse's *What Makes a Good School?*). Some TVEI consortia or clusters meet together and share a variety of INSET activities.

There is a strong case, however, for some of these days to be allocated to department or faculty teams.

Some teams will be further advanced in certain areas than others, and some will have particular strengths and weaknesses. An annual departmental review with Senior Management might be used to discuss these strengths and weaknesses, to set targets and to identify particular INSET needs. Advisers, Advisory teachers, outside consultants or other staff might then be used to support departments on these days.

Alternatively, some departments will be on the right lines and their biggest need will be time. It should be provided.

Differentiation in INSET is as important as differentiation in the classroom.

Finally, those responsible for introducing innovation must realise that in *getting started* all members of staff will have different levels of experience, expertise and confidence. The creation of an ethos of support, of praise and recognition will do more than any INSET activity to bring about real and lasting professional development.

APPENDIX   A Selected List of References

DART Directed Activities Related to Text from *Learning from the Written Word*. E Lunzer and K Gardner (1984) Oliver and Boyd.

RLDU Resources for Learning Development Unit, Sheridan Road, Horfield, Bristol BS7 OPU (0272 311105)

Skills for Adolescence TACADE 1 Hulme Place, The Crescent, Salford, M5 4QA

The following organisations can provide resources and information which will be of use to schools and colleges wishing to develop courses in open learning or supported self-study. Thanks are due to Colin Harris of BOLDU for providing this list.

BOLDU The National Open Learning Library at Birmingham Open Learning Development Unit, East Birmingham College, Garretts Green Lane, Birmingham B33 OTS (021 743 5236)

British Association for Open Learning Andrew Haldane, Staffordshire Open learning Unit, Chetwynd Centre, Newport Road, Stafford (0785 52313)

CSCS Centre for the Study of Comprehensive Schools Liza Griffith, CSCS, Wentworth College, University of York, York YO1 5DD (0904 433240)

Flexible Learning Newsletter Peter Trethewy, FEU, 2 Orange Street, London WC2 7WE (081 321 0433)

Flexible Learning Unit (TEED), St Mary's House, Moorfoot, Sheffield S1 4PQ (0742 593301)

LOCUST Chris McCallister, Cumbria Open Learning, College of Art and Technology, Brampton Road, Carlisle CA3 9AY (0228 512539)

LRDG David Scott, Learning Resources Development Group, Crewe and Alsager College, Hassall Road, Alsager ST7 2HL (0270 882500)

MARIS-NET (Ely) Ltd, 1 St Mary' Street, Ely, CB7 4ER Cambridgeshire (0353 661 284)

NASCL David Jackson, National Association for Student Centred Learning, 2 Church View, Norton-sub-Hamdon, Somerset TA14 6SG

NCET Julie Wright, Supported Self-Study Unit, National Council for Educational Technology Science Park, Warwick University, Coventry CV4 7EZ (0203 416994)

NEC National Extension College, 18 Brooklands Avenue, Cambridge CB2 2HN (0223 316644)

NATFHE Open Learning Section. Ian Hunter, Dunstable College, Kingsway, Dunstable LU5 4HG (90582 696451)

NERIS David Taylor, Maryland College, Leighton Street, Woburn, Milton Keynes MK17 9JD (0525 290364)

OLF Terry Watts, Open Learning Federation, Rawson House, 14 Edgeley Road, Countesthorpe, Leicester LE8 3QN (0533 774 591)

OLS News Anna Nichols, NCET/OLS News, 10 Metuchen Way, Hedge End, Southampton SO3 4JZ (042 121 4620)

OPEN UNIVERSITY PO Box 71, Walton Hall, Milton Keynes MK7 6AG (0908 653861)

INDEX

The Teaching and Learning Series

This book, *Resources for Flexible Learning,* is the third in the series and is closely related to four others which examine important issues both for the classroom teacher and the school or college manager.

Book 1, *Flexible Learning: an Outline*, by **Philip Waterhouse** provides an outline of all the key questions in the debate on teaching and learning styles. He examines the rationale, contexts and methods of *flexible learning*:

- The National Curriculum
- Assessment
- TVEI
- Records of Achievement
- Study skills

- Tutoring
- The flexible use of space, time, money and people
- The use of libraries and resource centres

Flexible Learning: an Outline is a **handbook**. Each chapter provides an agenda, a checklist of key issues and will be invaluable to all those interested in stimulating discussion or raising awareness on the subject of how teachers teach and how students learn.

ISBN 1 85539 003 5 £6.50

Book 2, *Classroom Management*, by **Philip Waterhouse**, provides a detailed insight into the management of a wide variety of teaching and learning strategies. It provides practical advice on:

- Planning and organisation of schemes of work
- Differentiation
- Assignments
- Management of resources
- The organisation and layout of classrooms
- Assessment and recording
- Managing the whole class, small group and individual work.

The book will be a valuable handbook for both classroom teachers and for those managing teaching and learning in schools and colleges.

ISBN 1 85539 004 3 £6.50

Book 4, *Tutoring*, by **Philip Waterhouse** explores the possibilities of skilful tutoring. It presents clearly:

- The rationale and objectives of tutoring
- The contexts for tutoring
- Arrangements for tutoring
- Tutoring styles
- Tutoring techniques.

The book will serve as an invaluable handbook for all those in schools and colleges seeking to provide guidance and support to students both in the classroom and in more informal learning situations.

ISBN 1 85539 006 X £6.50

Book 5, *What makes a Good School?* by **Tim Brighouse**, identifies those features of school organisation and management which are essential elements of successful teaching and learning. It examines:

- Leadership in the successful school
- Environment in the successful school
- Staff development in the successful school
- School and curriculum development planning
- The organisation of learning in the successful school
- Successful teaching and learning.

ISBN 1 85539 007 8 £6.50

This book is an introduction to a major series by Tim Brighouse (Research Machines Professor of Education, University of Keele) which explores each of the topics above in some depth. This series will be published by Network Educational Press.

All books in the *Teaching and Learning Series* £6.50. Discounts available for bulk orders direct from the publishers. Order forms and further details from:

Network Educational Press, PO Box 635, Stafford ST17 0JR

Telephone: 0785 225515

Other Titles from Network Educational Press

Coursework Enquiry/Study Guides
introduced by **Philip Waterhouse**

A series of photocopiable coursework enquiry/study guides is available in the following subject areas:

☐ Geography   ☐ Humanities   ☐ Business Studies

Each subject pack contains 30 different enquiries on a wide range of topics. The guides provide:

- clear, practical guidance
- advice on resources, activities and presentation
- scope for individual, group or class investigations
- flexibility in use.

60,000 of these guides have purchased by schools and colleges since their publication in May 1989. (The Geography pack was awarded the title **Best Secondary Text 1989** by the Geography Association.) The guides have been used in:

- Geography, Humanities and Business Studies (13-16)
- English (13-16)
- General Studies and PSE (14-18)
- CPVE and B TEC (16+).

Each pack £35.00.   A full set of Geography, Humanities and Business Studies £95.00. Brochures and order forms from the publishers.

Forthcoming Titles

The success of the study guides has led us to increase the range of subjects. During 1991, guides will be published in:

☐ Technology (from a range of   ☐ English Language
    disciplines)
                                         ☐ Science
☐ History
                                         ☐ Modern Languages

Details of all these publications from:

Network Educational Press, PO Box 635, Stafford ST17 0JR
Telephone: 0785 225515

English Literature

Activities / Assignments Guides

A series of photocopiable guides which support flexible styles of teaching and learning in English Literature.

☐ **16 titles in the range**

The guides provide a fresh and imaginative approach to English Literature and will appeal to:

- experienced teachers looking for new ideas
- teachers new to particular texts
- student teachers
- non-specialist teachers of English.

Each guide has three sections:

- a summary of key plot events (for easy reference)
- a collection of varied learning activities
- a collection of assignments.

The activities seek to develop a wide range of student skills:

- oral skills
- paired and small group work
- improvisation and role play
- discursive, narrative and creative writing.

The assignments engage the student in a detailed study of the text, are clearly differentiated, and seek to provide:

- a critical understanding of plot, character, and style
- suggestions for the open study or extension work
- scope for independent research
- coursework opportunities in English.

To be published Summer Term 1991 £24.00 per photocopiable pack of 16 titles. Available from the publishers:

**Network Educational Press, PO Box 635, Stafford ST17 0JR.
Telephone: 0785 225515**